Andover's Teaching and Departmental Reviews

Findings and Recommendations

HEATHER L. SCHWARTZ, ELIZABETH D. STEINER, REBECCA L. WOLFE,
DMITRY KHODYAKOV, EMILY DAO, DIANNE DOMENECH-BURGOS,
JEFFREY C. DOMINA, RAJESH R. MUNDRA

Sponsored by Phillips Academy Andover

Phillips Academy
ANDOVER

For more information on this publication, visit **www.rand.org/t/RRA1821-1**.

About RAND

The RAND Corporation is a research organization that develops solutions to public policy challenges to help make communities throughout the world safer and more secure, healthier and more prosperous. RAND is nonprofit, nonpartisan, and committed to the public interest. To learn more about RAND, visit www.rand.org.

Research Integrity

Our mission to help improve policy and decisionmaking through research and analysis is enabled through our core values of quality and objectivity and our unwavering commitment to the highest level of integrity and ethical behavior. To help ensure our research and analysis are rigorous, objective, and nonpartisan, we subject our research publications to a robust and exacting quality-assurance process; avoid both the appearance and reality of financial and other conflicts of interest through staff training, project screening, and a policy of mandatory disclosure; and pursue transparency in our research engagements through our commitment to the open publication of our research findings and recommendations, disclosure of the source of funding of published research, and policies to ensure intellectual independence. For more information, visit www.rand.org/about/research-integrity.

RAND's publications do not necessarily reflect the opinions of its research clients and sponsors.

Published by the RAND Corporation, Santa Monica, Calif.
© 2023 RAND Corporation
RAND® is a registered trademark.

Library of Congress Cataloging-in-Publication Data is available for this publication.

ISBN: 978-1-9774-1061-0

Cover image courtesy of Phillips Academy Andover

Limited Print and Electronic Distribution Rights

This publication and trademark(s) contained herein are protected by law. This representation of RAND intellectual property is provided for noncommercial use only. Unauthorized posting of this publication online is prohibited; linking directly to its webpage on rand.org is encouraged. Permission is required from RAND to reproduce, or reuse in another form, any of its research products for commercial purposes. For information on reprint and reuse permissions, please visit www.rand.org/pubs/permissions.

About This Report

To update its teaching and departmental review processes, Phillips Academy Andover, an independent boarding school in Andover, Massachusetts, commissioned the RAND Corporation in 2021 to review its policies, conduct a literature review, interview other independent high schools, develop potential recommendations for revision of Andover's processes, and then revise those recommendations after vetting them with Andover's faculty. This report summarizes RAND's work.

The report is intended primarily for Andover administrators and teachers to guide their revision of their teaching and departmental review processes, but we also hope it will be a resource for other independent schools. To help readers understand how proposed changes may or may not work in different contexts, we include in this report Andover teachers' reactions to initial potential recommendations, our subsequent revisions to the recommendations based on their feedback, and Andover administrators' reactions to our final recommendations.

RAND Education and Labor

This study was undertaken by RAND Education and Labor, a division of the RAND Corporation that conducts research on early childhood through postsecondary education programs, workforce development, and programs and policies affecting workers, entrepreneurship, and financial literacy and decisionmaking. This study was funded by Phillips Academy Andover, an independent, coeducational secondary school with an expansive worldview and a legacy of academic excellence.

More information about RAND can be found at www.rand.org. Questions about this report should be directed to heather_schwartz@rand.org, and questions about RAND Education and Labor should be directed to educationandlabor@rand.org.

Acknowledgments

We are grateful to the Andover faculty who provided generous amounts of time to participate in this project. Their honesty, detailed feedback, and participation were essential to shaping the recommendations we ultimately posed. We also thank Katherine Carman, Doug Ward and Alice Huguet for their helpful reviews of this report; they greatly improved this report. We also thank Emily Haglund for document support, Emily Dao for supporting the ExpertLens survey, James Torr for his editorial expertise, and Monette Velasco for overseeing the publication process for this report.

Summary

Unlike public kindergarten through 12th grade (K–12) and postsecondary schools, independent schools have scant relevant research to inform their design of teaching and departmental review policies. Phillips Academy Andover (hereafter called Andover), an independent boarding school in Andover, Massachusetts, enlisted the RAND Corporation, a nonprofit and nonpartisan research organization, to research existing practices and recommend new processes for departmental review and for teaching review. Departmental reviews entail setting instructional goals and then ensuring that the curriculum, teaching, and student assessment align with those goals. Teaching reviews here refer to a developmental process for giving feedback to teachers about their teaching and to set goals for growth, as opposed to a managerial process to determine salary or employment status.

Andover requested this independent review from RAND in response to two internal studies it had conducted. The first was a 2019 self-study to prepare for its reaccreditation visit. This self-study noted the absence of an explicit school-wide curriculum plan. The second was the initial findings of the school's Anti-Racist Taskforce from 2020 that highlighted the need for more formal documentation of performance expectations and reviews, job descriptions, and operational guidelines for departments at the school. In addition to reviewing the literature on teaching and departmental review processes from public K–12 schools and postsecondary institutions, we reviewed Andover documents, interviewed current and former Andover department chairs about how the school's current policies work in practice, interviewed other K–12 independent schools, developed a set of draft recommendations for revising Andover's teaching and departmental reviews, and collected Andover faculty ratings and feedback about these potential recommendations using a modified Delphi-method. Each of these data sources informed our ultimate recommendations.

This report is primarily intended as a reference tool for Andover's administrators and teachers who serve on the committees charged with updating the school's teaching and departmental review policies and documentation. Therefore, we start Chapters 2–4 with key takeaways so that committee members can quickly learn what they need to know and then jump to later sections in the chapter as needed. This summary provides an overview of the report for all Andover staff, faculty, and trustees.

We hope that this report will also be a resource for other independent schools that are considering changes to their teaching or departmental review processes. The interviews we conducted at other independent schools lead us to believe that many independent schools share similar challenges related to teaching reviews as Andover. We hope that the extensive literature review, the explanation of how our recommendations evolved in response to Andover faculty reactions, and Andover administrators' own reactions to our revised recommendations will provide other independent schools with useful ideas and help them consider potential faculty and administrator reaction to potential revisions to their policies.

To set the stage for our recommendations, we first explain in Chapter 2 Andover's current teaching review, which is for professional growth and does not determine salary, and departmental review process as designed and as practiced. We then summarize in Chapter 3 the published research as well as information from independent schools we interviewed about the various elements of teaching and departmental reviews. Then—because Andover's revisions to its teaching and departmental review processes need to fit the school's context to succeed, and because teacher and administrator buy-in is crucial to the ultimate success of any system for teaching and departmental review—we detail Andover teachers' and administrators' reactions (positive and negative) to our initial and then revised recommendations. We view Andover teachers' reactions (in Chapter 4) as well as administrators' reactions (in Chapter 6) as being equally important as the recommendations themselves (in Chapter 5).

Key Findings

- The principles of Andover's current teaching review system are sound in that they are consistent with prior research.
- However, the school does not consistently conduct its intended annual informal teaching reviews. It does conduct the periodic, formal reviews for the most part.
- There is a strong foundation from which to build a more coherent instructional system at Andover. For example, some departments have already identified a set of student learning objectives and aligned their course content across years and within courses. Also, Andover faculty are eager to engage in departmental conversations about instructional improvement and observe their colleagues' teaching.
- Like many other independent schools, Andover does not articulate clear goals for student learning in each department and across the school. Explicit goals for student learning are the starting point for a more coherent instructional system, as departments can then determine whether they offer courses that build year-on-year in a coherent and comprehensive fashion such that the instruction students receive over the course of (up to) four years covers Andover's full set of desired learning objectives. Likewise, the lack of a common instructional vision may also undermine the clarity and purpose of the teaching review system. At its worst, a lack of clarity about expectations can create potentially inequitable conditions for teachers.
- Andover teachers endorsed eight of our 14 potential recommendations over the course of a three-round vetting process. These included the identification of desired student competencies, a more frequent and department chair-led teaching review, annual department-led self-studies, and revision of the school-wide student survey. Faculty did not endorse the idea of instructional coaches leading teaching reviews (instead preferring that department chairs lead this process), and they were uncertain whether either identifying desired teaching competencies or inviting external observers to review their department would be helpful for their teaching.
- A running theme through teachers' responses was a strong preference for department-initiated processes over centralized, school-wide processes, and a desire to preserve instructors' individual autonomy. Faculty conveyed skepticism about the practicality or benefit of taking a top-down approach to crafting or revising departmental or teaching review policy.

Our Recommendations

We recommend that Andover enact the following changes, which we have organized into two major themes. In response to Andover faculty feedback, we reoriented our recommendations to take a more bottom-up approach, because Andover teachers strongly endorsed departments rather than school-wide committees as the most trusted and effective place to discuss and review teaching.

Recommendation 1: Andover should engage faculty in a multi-year process to improve the coherence of its instructional system

Our research suggests that Andover should state clear and shared learning expectations for students so that teachers know what they are aiming for and what they are expected to do. Andover leaders themselves noted this lack of shared instructional vision in the school's 2019 self-study and the school's accreditors concurred in their 2022 review. Each department creating learning expectations for students that funnel into a shared school-wide set of expectations lays the groundwork for departments to then maintain a high-quality curriculum that covers the desired topics and skills, assessments that are aligned to the curriculum, and professional learning for teachers that is aligned to the curriculum. The last stage in the recurring sequence of a coherent instructional system is a teaching review that provides feedback to teachers about their teaching in light of the shared expectations for student learning.

To design a more coherent instructional system we propose that Andover, like other independent schools that have embarked on a similar project, engage faculty in this work over four or more years. We recommend the following steps:

1. In the first year, Andover should articulate what skills and competencies it wishes students to acquire over the course of their time at Andover.
2. In the second year, each department should refresh, create, or re-approve its curriculum map, which visualizes what is being taught in each department and at each grade or course level, and outlines the relationships within and between the courses in a program of study.
3. In the third year, Andover should revise faculty job expectations in its *General Policies Handbook* and the *Faculty and Administrator Supplement* to the *General Policies Handbook*. We suggest that departments first suggest updates to these to make the expectations of teachers clearer.
4. In the fourth year, Andover should revise its guidance and materials for the annual informal reviews and periodic formal reviews to tie the teacher evaluation process more directly to the instructional system. For example, Andover should create a guide for annual conversations between chairs and teachers, including a prompt to discuss which student skills or competencies the teacher is building.

Recommendation 2: Andover should focus on simplifying and fully implementing its ten guiding principles for teaching review

We endorse the ten guiding principles that Andover faculty adopted in 2017 for the school's teaching evaluation system, as the principles align with the research. Working from these principles, Andover should develop a more streamlined process and provide chairs with more training, guidance, and ideally a reduced workload to allow them to implement the teaching reviews fully and well. Our recommendations in this second category thus center on operations:

1. Andover should require that all department chairs hold annual individual conversations of at least 30 minutes with their faculty (i.e., annual informal reviews). These would be conversations in which teachers and department chairs can set goals for the year for that teacher and discuss goals from the prior year. We recommend that the school revisit chair responsibilities to free up time for the annual conversations.
2. Andover should retain a simplified version of its chair-led formal teaching review process, but we recommend that the process occur every six years rather than every eight. A six-year frequency means that a department chair, who has a six-year term, would formally review each faculty member once.
3. Andover should purchase an online documentation system for performance reviews in which notes from the annual conversations and the elements of the periodic formal teacher reviews would be housed. Teachers would have full access to their own account, as would relevant administrators.
4. To provide logistical support and training, Andover should hire a full-time project manager to oversee Andover's faculty review processes and ensure that reviews happen on time. This is consistent with the other independent schools we interviewed. This project manager could train chairs in concert with others about the annual and periodic feedback process, oversee the development of written procedural guidance, work with departments' administrative assistants to ensure that chairs have annual conversations with each faculty member, notify teachers when they are scheduled for formal

reviews, oversee the online documentation system, and oversee the school-wide student survey administration.
5. To encourage full implementation, we recommend that Andover streamline several aspects of its informal and formal reviews.
    a. Eliminate the Annual Performance Review Form, which department chairs reported they largely do not use. Instead, department chairs should type free-form notes in the online documentation system during informal, annual goal-setting conversations with teachers.
    b. Although the specifics are outside our scope, we also recommend simplifying and streamlining the residential, advising, and athletic reviews that are a part of the formal reviews to make the process less time-consuming and easier to enact.
    c. Reduce the time required for the formal academic teaching review by dropping the two peer observations and three evaluation committee member observations (which are in addition to the one observation by the department or division chair). In lieu of the peer observation, we suggest instituting an expectation that each faculty member observe at least one class per year by a fellow faculty member in their department as part of their department's self-study.
    d. Add teacher-introduced classroom artifact(s) and/or lesson plans as one of the multiple measures in a formal review. In the spirit of organizing the formal review around substantive discussion of instruction and pedagogy, teachers could accompany their written reflection with examples of student work, lesson plans, or results from one of the faculty member's student surveys to illustrate an instructional activity or exercise that follows from one of the teacher's goals.
    a. Revamp the school-wide student survey and do not use it as an element of the teaching review. We offer several detailed suggestions in Chapter 5, but the main idea is to split the current survey in two: (1) all faculty members should field their own surveys of their students at least once per year about questions of the faculty member's choosing (this is already common practice at the school); (2) the school should field a shorter, anonymous survey *focused on factually oriented questions to ensure basic course functions occur as intended in each class.*
6. We recommend training for all faculty about the revised teaching review and departmental review policies, along with more intensive training for department chairs. This training would include awareness of and ways to reduce bias in the informal and formal reviews.

Table S.1 brings all these recommendations together by placing the school's current practices alongside our recommendations.

Finally, we suggest that Andover administrators and teachers keep four principles in mind as they decide which of these recommendations to adopt, modify, or reject. We draw these common-sense principles from research about implementing school reforms.

- Principle 1: Teacher buy-in is essential to successful change. As they did when designing the current system, Andover administrators can gain buy-in by taking a collaborative approach in which teachers are involved in the design of new systems and processes. Administrators can also increase buy-in by taking an iterative approach to policy design in which ideas are generated using both bottom-up and top-down approaches, tested in pilot projects, and adopted in phases. Clear communication along the way about the change efforts through multiple channels (i.e., email, department meetings, all-staff meetings, new staff trainings) is also important.
- Principle 2: Give faculty and departments time to meet to do the work of collating existing resources, identifying student competencies, and engaging in departmental review activities. Providing adequate time for meaningful collaboration has the additional benefit of strengthening professional ties and fac-

TABLE S.1
Summary of Andover's Current Policies and Our Recommendations

Activity	Current Process	Recommendation
Departmental reviews	• Andover encourages departmental reviews, but does not have formal guidance or requirements about them.	• Andover should require that each department engage in a self-study each year. • Departments can be the engine for a multi-year process in which Andover creates a more coherent instructional system. • Every six years, each department should revisit its desired student competencies and its curriculum map. • Each year, each department should discuss the self-study topic with the Dean of Studies and report at the end of the year about the outcomes. • As a part of self-studies, each faculty should observe at least one class of a faculty person within their department each year.

Teaching review	• Chairs are to meet each year with faculty to conduct an informal review, but this largely does not happen.
	• Formal reviews occur in the third and eighth year of a teachers' tenure at Andover, then every eight years thereafter. Department chairs lead the formal reviews.
	• The teaching review process is guided by eight principles.
	• The teaching review theoretically includes the school-wide student survey, but the results are largely not useful.
		• The teaching reviews should be one element of a coherent instructional system that starts with departments and the school identifying desired student competencies.
		• Andover should keep its eight guiding principles, enforce them, and retain a department-chair led teaching review process.
		  – Specifically, chairs or assistant chairs should meet with each faculty for at least 30 minutes each year.
		  – Andover should simplify its processes to make them easier to implement.
		  – Also to reduce burden, Andover should retain only the department chair observation within the formal teaching review and drop the Evaluation Committee and peer review observations.
		  – Add teacher-introduced classroom artifact(s) and/or lesson plans as one of the multiple measures in the formal review.
		• Andover should eliminate or replace its teaching review forms and instead adopt an online documentation system to which both the teacher and department chair have access.
		• Andover should hire a project manager to ensure that the informal and formal teaching reviews occur as intended and to reduce burden on chairs in particular.
		• Also to reduce burden, Andover should retain only the department chair observation within the formal teaching review and drop the Evaluation Committee and peer review observations.
		• Andover should provide training to teachers and more extended training to chairs about enacting the teaching review.

ulty buy-in, although we recognize that some faculty could perceive it as an additional obligation in an already busy schedule.

- Principle 3: Institutional commitment is crucial and can promote faculty buy-in. Institutional commitment can include strong leadership, resources (such as course relief, or other sources of time) to accomplish the work, compensation for additional work, and administrative or project management resources.
- Principle 4: Complexity lowers the likelihood of implementation. A simple process entails tools that are relatively quick to train staff to use, that are easy to use in practice, and that require a reasonable and therefore sustainable time commitment required from department chairs and from faculty—ideally no more than a couple of hours per faculty member receiving a formal review rather than the 5–12 hours that chairs estimated they currently take.

Limitations of Our Analysis

There are several limitations of our analysis. The first is a notable lack of published research about the design, implementation, or effects of independent schools' teaching or departmental evaluation systems. We draw on public K–12 and postsecondary research instead in our literature review, noting which aspects are and are not relevant to independent high school settings such as Andover.

Because of the lack of published research, we relied on interviews to gather information about independent schools. We talked with a limited number of other independent schools (eight schools plus four networks of independent schools), so we do not have a complete view of how all of Andover's peer schools conduct their teaching reviews and departmental reviews. We purposely sought out schools that were reputed to have high-quality teaching or departmental reviews or had at least initiated a revision to their review system to learn what changes they made and why.

Finally, we conducted this work during the COVID-19 pandemic school year of 2021–2022. Department chairs were recalling teaching evaluation practices from 18 months earlier because Andover suspended the teaching review activities during the pandemic. While we interviewed all 28 current and former department or division chairs we approached and therefore had information about each department, Andover teacher participation rates in the three-round process in which we solicited feedback on our draft recommendations were lower than we would have liked. We invited all 158 teaching faculty to anonymously rate and discuss potential RAND recommendations to revise Andover's teaching and departmental review policies, and 63 percent did so in the first round. But only 39 percent did so by the third and final round. Therefore, the teacher views we summarize in the final round may not represent the views of all Andover teachers.

Although the demographic characteristics of the teachers who participated in round 3 generally matched the demographic profile of the faculty overall, the largest difference was an overrepresentation of veteran faculty (those with 10 or more years of experience at Andover; 69 percent of round 3 participants versus 57 percent of the overall teaching faculty). Thus, faculty with less than a decade of experience at Andover were underrepresented. White faculty were also somewhat overrepresented in round 3 (75 percent of round 3 participants versus 69 percent of faculty overall) and faculty of color were underrepresented (25 percent of round 3 participants versus 31 percent overall). In short, we cannot know whether the views we summarize are systematically different than the views of the Andover teachers overall. However, we think that their feedback, although not necessarily representative of all Andover teachers, is an important source of information that Andover administrators should consider as the school revises its teaching and departmental reviews.

Contents

About This Report.. iii
Summary.. v
Figures and Tables.. xiii

CHAPTER 1
Introduction... 1

CHAPTER 2
Andover's Teaching and Departmental Reviews as Designed and Practiced.................................. 3
    Key Takeaways.. 3
    Overview of Andover's Teaching Evaluation Policy.. 4
    Detail About the Periodic Formal Teaching Reviews.. 5
    Detail About the Informal, Annual Teaching Reviews 8
    Detail About the School-Wide Student Survey 10
    Andover's Departmental Review Processes 12

CHAPTER 3
The Research About Teaching and Departmental Reviews as Applied to Independent Schools............ 15
    Key Takeaways.. 15
    What's the Goal? Schools Should Have Coherent Instructional Systems to Promote Consistent
        Student Academic Experiences 16
    Academic Departments as the Engine of a Coherent Instructional System 16
    Teaching Evaluation Systems as a Part of a Larger, Coherent Instructional System 23
    Making a Coherent Instructional System Work in Practice 35

CHAPTER 4
Andover Faculty Views About Potential Policy Revisions... 39
    Key Takeaways.. 39
    Participation Rates... 40
    Results from Rounds 1 and 2 41
    Results from Round 3... 46
    Summary of the Recommendations Faculty Endorsed 51

CHAPTER 5
Recommendations... 53
    Start a Multi-Year Process to Design a Coherent Instructional System 53
    Focus on Full Execution of Andover's Ten Guiding Principles for Teaching Reviews, and Simplify
        Some Processes to Reach That Goal 55

CHAPTER 6
Andover's Reactions to the Recommendations... 61
    Student Competencies... 62
    Teaching Reviews 63
    Department Reviews.. 64

APPENDIXES
A. Methods 67
B. Andover's Statement of Purpose, Values, and Academic Vision 87

Abbreviations 89
References 91

Figures and Tables

Figures

4.1.	Distribution of Faculty Ratings from Round 3	47
A.1.	How a Potential Recommendation Appeared in Round 1 of ExpertLens	74
A.2.	How the Results for a Potential Recommendation Appeared in Round 2 of ExpertLens	75
A.3.	How the Anonymous Discussion Board Appeared in Round 2 of ExpertLens	76
A.4.	How a Revised Recommendation Appeared in Round 3 of ExpertLens	76
A.5.	Algorithm to Calculate Panel Decisions in ExpertLens	77

Tables

S.1.	Summary of Andover's Current Policies and Our Recommendations	ix
3.1.	Characteristics of Commonly Used Observation Tools for High School Level	28
4.1.	Faculty Participation in Three Rounds of ExpertLens	40
4.2.	Participation Rates by Faculty Demographic Categories	40
4.3.	Faculty Ratings in Round 1 About the Helpfulness of a Policy Change for Their Teaching	42
4.4.	Faculty Reactions to Six Questions About Ways to Modify the Most Controversial Proposed Changes from Round 1	43
4.5.	Faculty Ratings from Round 3 About the Helpfulness of a Policy Change for Their Teaching	46
4.6.	Faculty Subgroup Round 3 Determinations and Median Rating About the Helpfulness of a Policy Change for Their Teaching	49
4.7.	Themes in Faculty Comments from Round 3	50
4.8.	The Eight Recommendations Andover Teachers Deemed Helpful	51
5.1.	Summary of Andover's Current Policies and RAND's Recommendations	59
A.1.	Andover Department Chair Interviewees	70
A.2.	Faculty Ratings of Helpfulness and Feasibility of 14 Potential Recommendations in Round 1	78
A.3.	Faculty Ratings of Helpfulness of Potential Recommendations in Round 3	83

CHAPTER 1

Introduction

Founded in 1778, Phillips Academy Andover (hereafter called Andover) is a large independent school that enrolls about 1,200 students in grades 9 through 12. It is one the oldest and most prestigious secondary schools in the United States. As a boarding school, Andover serves a highly diverse student body—about half of whom are students of color—who come from 47 countries and 41 of the 50 United States.

Andover employs approximately 150 permanent teaching faculty, plus additional temporary teacher fellows who serve several-year terms. Over time, the school has increasingly formalized its teacher review policies to include either a brief, informal annual review or a more elaborate formal review that occurs in the third and eighth year of teaching at Andover, and then every eight years thereafter. The formal teaching review incorporates the numerous roles that teachers play at Andover and includes their academic, athletic, residential, and advising duties. (The school runs a separate, annual review for non-teaching staff.) The school had last enacted a major internal update of its teaching review system in 2015. Before that, the last time academic departments and the curriculum were reviewed was in 1978.

In 2019, the school completed a self-study to prepare for its accreditor's visit (New England Association of Schools and Colleges [NEASC]) and found that Andover lacked a school-wide curriculum plan, that program evaluations were not always clear across campus (or across departments), and that teacher autonomy led to substantial variation in pedagogical and assessment practices.

Thereafter, the school started in 2020 to examine how to better coordinate the self-study and review activities in which academic departments independently engage. Historically, the school's 19 departments and their faculty have had substantial autonomy. This history of strong teacher autonomy reflects the faculty's considerable academic qualifications and experience; about 27 percent of the teaching faculty hold doctorates and 57 percent have taught at the school for at least a decade.

NEASC confirmed the high degree of faculty autonomy and lack of common planning, while also offering high praise for the school's renowned offerings. In its 2021 visiting committee report (not available to the general public), the NEASC team wrote that "At every turn, we were impressed with the wealth and quality of classes, activities, and resources available to students. From theater and music rehearsals to class discussions to athletics to club meetings, we saw overwhelming evidence of the power and beauty of a Phillips Academy education" (p. 26). Where the NEASC visiting committee saw flaws was in "less evidence of a shared understanding [among Andover faculty] of the planning process," and committee counseled that the school "create and embrace a comprehensive curricular plan" (p. 8).

In the same year as the NEASC report, Andover's Anti-Racism Task Force, which was formed to address the inequities people of color have faced at the school, also highlighted in its initial findings the need for the school to look again at its faculty evaluation system to ensure it is equitable for all faculty.

In response to these reports, the headmaster decided to obtain an independent review of the academic teaching review process of its permanent teaching faculty and to obtain recommendations about departmental reviews. In late 2021, the school enlisted the services of the RAND Corporation, a nonprofit, nonpartisan research organization, to research and recommend new processes for departmental review and for teaching evaluation. This report summarizes our review.

We performed an extensive literature review, interviewed the school's department chairs and eight other U.S. independent schools, and engaged Andover's teachers in a three-round online feedback process to obtain and then discuss their ratings and comments about potential changes to Andover's teaching and departmental review processes. This report summarizes the results of that work and provides RAND's ensuing recommendations for the school.

While the report is primarily for Andover administrators and teachers, we also believe it can be useful for other independent schools for three reasons. First, our interviews of leaders from independent schools suggest that many face similar challenges to balance teacher autonomy with clear, well-executed systems of review. Second, we hope the literature review will be of wide use for independent schools. Third, the inclusion of our initial recommendations, Andover teaching faculty's reaction to them, our resulting revisions, and Andover administrators' reactions to our final recommendations will hopefully shed light on the all-important stage where the recipients (in this case, Andover faculty and administrators) adopt, adapt, or reject third-party recommendations to fit local context. This stage is rarely reported, and we hope that this information will help other schools as they anticipate the likely reception or applicability of the recommendations in their own settings.

In the chapters that follow, we first explain Andover's teaching review and department review policies and how those policies operate in practice according to the school's department chairs. We then provide in Chapter 3 a literature review and the results of our interviews of other independent schools about elements of departmental and teaching reviews, highlighting where the research is and is not conclusive. We used the literature review, independent school interviews, and department chair feedback to form potential recommendations for changes that we asked Andover faculty to rate. These potential recommendations are presented in Chapter 4, along with faculty's ratings of them. In Chapter 4 we also highlight common themes in teachers' written reactions to help inform Andover's future committees as they revise their teaching evaluation and departmental review policies. In Chapter 5, we present our final recommendations. To summarize, Chapters 1–5 contain our research and analysis. In Chapter 6, we conclude with Andover's reactions to the recommendations, which three Andover administrators wrote.

CHAPTER 2

Andover's Teaching and Departmental Reviews as Designed and Practiced

In this chapter we summarize Andover's teaching review and departmental review policies[1] both as they are designed and as they are actually implemented according to Andover department chairs, who lead both types of reviews.[2] We note that our scope included only the review of academic teaching (and not the advising, residential, and athletic reviews) for permanent teaching faculty. Therefore, this chapter does not include Andover's review of teaching fellows and staff, who are evaluated via a different set of policies. Throughout the report, we refer to Andover's policy as a *teaching review* rather than a *teacher evaluation*, because the term *evaluation* conjures a high-stakes system, which the school does not have. In contrast to a high-stakes evaluation, in which salary actions and employment decisions are directly tied to the outcome, Andover's teaching review is a developmental tool intended to help faculty reflect on and improve their teaching practices.

Key Takeaways

- Andover's principles for its teaching review system are sound and consistent with prior research.
- The lack of training and scant documentation about teaching reviews and departmental reviews creates inconsistency across the school and can create worry for faculty about the purpose of the teaching review in particular.
- Andover does not have a written policy for departmental self-reviews, and the processes that department chairs described were organic, informal, and largely driven by the chair.
- Department chairs reported that the intended annual conversations with each faculty do not occur for the most part, but that the periodic formal reviews do.
- The most complicated parts of the teaching review processes (such as faculty selecting from a menu of professional development activities each year) are the ones least likely to be implemented.
- We note a strong preference in department chair interviews for department-initiated processes over centralized, Andover-wide processes.

---

[1] Our summary of Andover's teaching evaluation policy comes primarily from the current version of the *Faculty Evaluation Handbook* and a 2015 Faculty Evaluation Committee report that was the basis for that handbook's policies.

[2] In October–November 2021, we interviewed either the current or former chair (or both) of each academic department at Andover. We interviewed former chairs in departments where the current chair had not yet led formal teacher reviews because Andover had suspended its normal teaching evaluation practices during the COVID-19 pandemic. In all, we interviewed 28 current or former chairs, of which 11 had started as chair in 2019–2020 or later. We explain our methods for the interviews in the technical appendix.

Overview of Andover's Teaching Evaluation Policy

Andover's teaching review policy consists of three parts:

1. A formal review in the teacher's third year at Andover, eighth year at Andover, and then every eight years thereafter. The formal review has several parts, including six classroom observations as we discuss below.
2. An annual informal review that is a conversation between the department chair and each individual teacher in the department. Once a faculty member has been formally reviewed (see #2 next), the faculty person is to select one activity per year (e.g., participate in a pedagogy pod, videotape their class and review it) for professional development.
3. An annual school-wide survey of students. Each teacher is to administer this survey in November, and the results are intended to inform both the informal and formal reviews.

Because the teaching review is intended to emphasize professional growth and development to improve instructional practice, the annual and periodic faculty teaching reviews do not have explicit or direct implications for salary or continued employment. Instead, any performance concerns that emerge during a review are to be discussed with the faculty member, the department chair, and Dean of Faculty and Dean of Studies, who together develop a professional learning plan that sits outside the annual or periodic review process.

An Andover committee composed of eight faculty members designed this three-part teaching review policy in 2015. Faculty voted to adopt it, and it is set forth in Andover's *Faculty Evaluation Handbook*. The Dean of Faculty formed the committee, named the Evaluation Review Committee, in 2013 and tasked it with revising Andover's student feedback survey and suggesting revisions to Andover's faculty evaluation system. Prior to this 2015 revision, the teaching review process had not been revised since 1978. According to our interviews of department chairs in 2021, it was widely understood that the older system from the 1970s was not being implemented with fidelity, as faculty were not being evaluated at the intended intervals.

As a result of the Evaluation Review Committee's work, Andover faculty also voted in 2015 to approve the following ten guiding principles for the faculty evaluation process, which we quote from the Evaluation Committee's report:

1. Faculty evaluation will be founded on and guided by the philosophy that the primary purpose of the process is to provide an opportunity for professional growth and development.
2. The basis for evaluation will be clear, written job expectations, as outlined in a job description and/or as outlined in the *General Policies Handbook* and the *Faculty and Administrator Supplement* to the *General Policies Handbook*.
3. Evaluation procedures will operate in accordance with the non-discrimination policy and apply consistently to all teaching faculty and administrative faculty.
4. The evaluation system will employ the use of multiple measures to assess performance.
5. The evaluation system will be based on established, well-respected research and best practices.
6. The evaluation system will acknowledge the existence of biases, both intentional and unintentional, and include measures to address such biases.
7. Evaluators will have training, specific guidelines, and support.
8. Faculty will be evaluated on schedule, balancing the need for regular feedback, and a sustainable process.
9. Faculty members will have access to all summary materials included in their evaluation file and have recourse for appeal.
10. The evaluation system will be reviewed at least every eight years.

In June 2015, the Evaluation Review Committee published a report that provided guidance to the faculty about the evaluation process, and recommended annual evaluation training for all department chairs and follow-up evaluation training for new administrators, and recommended the school provide students with guidance about how to provide constructive feedback. Almost all department chairs, however, told us they did not complete the informal annual reviews, nor did they recall receiving training about the periodic or annual teaching reviews. Nor has there been a more concerted (school-wide) effort to cultivate student capacity to provide valuable feedback, like a standardized script to be read by the teacher prior to administering the student survey.

In the rest of this chapter, we detail the intended and actual informal and formal teaching review, the annual student survey, and departmental reviews. We also note which aspects of the reviews department chairs think are and are not working well, and what they would like to see change.

Detail About the Periodic Formal Teaching Reviews

Written Policy

On a staggered schedule, each teaching faculty member is supposed to undergo a periodic formal teaching review. The first formal review is to occur during a faculty member's third year of teaching at Andover, then during their eighth year, and then every eight years thereafter (teaching year 16, year 24, etc.). The process starts in the fall and ends in the spring and involves a teaching review led primarily by the department chair. The process also includes a review led by the athletic director, an advising review led by the Dean of Studies for advising, and, for house counselors, a residential review led by the cluster dean. By spring, the department chair is to compile all four sources of reviews and submit them to the Dean of Faculty and Dean of Studies.

Here we describe only the formal academic teaching review. According to Andover's *Faculty Evaluation Handbook*, the academic component of the overall formal teaching review process should be completed within one trimester.[3] We describe each of these activities in the rough order in which they are to be completed:

- **Pre-evaluation meeting.** Faculty members should first meet with their department or division chair in the fall to review the process, set a timeline for completing required activities, and select a peer observer.
- **Written personal statement.** The faculty member being reviewed should write a personal statement. This statement is an opportunity for reflection in which the faculty member should describe their roles and responsibilities at Andover, and areas of strength and room for improvement. They should also update their professional goals. The written statement should ideally be completed before classroom observations occur. The faculty member is expected to share the written statement with classroom observers before the observation.
- **Classroom observations.** Each faculty member should be observed at least six times during the one trimester. At least two of these observations should be conducted by a peer observer,[4] three by an evaluation committee member,[5] and one by the department or division chair. Peer observers and evaluation committee members should hold brief conferences with the faculty member before and after each observation. The pre-conference meeting is intended to be a time in which the faculty member can share any necessary context about the lesson being observed or specific things they would like the advisor to look

---

[3] Andover operates on a trimester system; a term, or trimester, is about ten weeks.

[4] Peer is not defined, and in some departments chairs said faculty can pick any teacher at Andover, and in other departments chairs said the peer must be from within the department.

[5] There are six evaluation committee members who were assigned to this role. They received workload credit for this work.

for. The post-conference meeting is intended to be a time in which the observer and the faculty member can debrief from the observation and share developmental feedback. Observations may be announced or unannounced. Observers are expected to keep Andover's four dimensions of teaching practice in mind during their observation, take notes, and complete the short Classroom Observation Form, which the Evaluation Review Committee designed and is included in the *Faculty Evaluation Handbook*. Either the peer observer or the evaluation committee member doing the observation should be in a different department from the person being evaluated.

- **School-wide student feedback surveys.** Faculty are expected to administer Andover's online student feedback survey to the students in their classes in the last few weeks of the first trimester of the school year. We discuss these surveys in more detail later in this chapter.
- **Meeting with department chair.** After all the above activities have been completed the faculty member and department chair should meet. Prior to this meeting the faculty person should ensure that the department chair has all the relevant materials from the above activities (e.g., student feedback survey results, classroom observation forms, written personal statement), and the department chair should review these materials. This meeting is intended to be a holistic conversation about and reflection on the faculty member's teaching that year and identify areas of strength and areas for improvement. After this conversation, the department chair should complete the Annual Performance Review Form and assemble the full package of materials to share with the Dean of Faculty.
- **Meeting with Dean of Faculty and Dean of Studies (or corresponding senior leadership team administrator).** This is the final activity in the teaching review process. The Dean of Faculty reviews the department chair's summary and the student feedback survey results and meets with the faculty member being reviewed to discuss areas of strength, areas for development, and professional learning activities.

Practice

Department chairs rotate every six years, and Andover suspended teaching reviews due to COVID-19 during 2020 and 2021. Therefore, department chairs we spoke to in fall 2021 were describing processes that had last taken place about 18 months earlier. In fact, most of the most of the 11 current department chairs told us they had not yet conducted formal reviews of faculty because their term as chair began just before, or just after, the beginning of the pandemic. Instead, these current chairs described the formal teaching review process they experienced as faculty members. Because of new chairs' limited experience with conducting teaching reviews, we also interviewed former chairs from those 11 departments led by new chairs.

Most chairs described a formal review process that included a written reflection, classroom observations from the department chair, a peer observer, and member of the evaluation committee, pre- and post-observation meetings, and a summative conversation with the Dean of Faculty. Chairs agreed that observations were announced. Most chairs noted that formal reviews were periodic, with the first review happening in the third year of teaching. Chairs confirmed that Andover did not have an electronic database or system for documenting formal reviews. A few current chairs said that they received an email notifying them of their upcoming formal evaluation (as faculty) and explaining the process; no former chairs mentioned this.

However, some of the details of the process outlined in the *Faculty Evaluation Handbook* were reportedly inconsistently implemented. For example, the number of observations chairs described ranged from three total (e.g., one from each observer) to five or six (e.g., one or two from each observer). Some chairs described post-observation conferences that involved a discussion of feedback while others said that they received quick emails or received verbal feedback from observers in short conversations. Few chairs mentioned pre-observation conferences.

Chairs (many of which were newly appointed during the pandemic years) were mixed on whether there were restrictions on who could be a peer observer: some said there were no restrictions, others said the peer observer should be someone outside the department, and still others said the peer observer should be someone from within the department or division. Few chairs were aware of the observation form, and only three said they used it regularly.

Chairs varied in when the self-assessment was supposed to be written—some reported that it should be written at the beginning of the review process, while others said it was the last activity before meeting with the Dean of Faculty. None of the chairs we interviewed, past or present, said they had received training about the observation process, but most would have found such training useful.

These interviews revealed two main challenges related to implementing the formal review process as designed. First, the review process was perceived to be too time-consuming and burdensome. Several chairs noted that it was difficult to schedule observations (their own and the peer observers'), while others noted that delays in submitting materials from different people at different stages of the process—including the athletic, residential, and advisory reviews—caused the overall process to take longer than designed. For example, one chair said that their inputs to the Dean of Faculty could not be submitted until they had received input from all the observers and the faculty member under review. Thus, a delay by the peer observer caused a cascade of delays that ultimately caused many reviews to take longer than a single term. One reason for such delays could be (as one chair said) that the review process is not a priority for faculty; another could be because it is legitimately time-consuming in light of a faculty member's other responsibilities.

Nine chairs estimated the time they spend reviewing one faculty member. Their estimates ranged from five to 12 hours per faculty member. One chair said, "It's hard to evaluate people who are doing complex jobs that have lots of tasks…we have four to five jobs, and the classroom part is one piece, and it's a lot of work. The evaluation is well intended and they [administrators] want it to be growth-oriented, but it's tons of logistics. It would be great to streamline the process."

Chairs also noted that frequency of the formal teaching reviews deviated from the intended schedule after the first review in the third year of teaching. However, some were commenting on their experience of the pre-2015 system, which we were told was serially behind in initiating the periodic reviews. One chair, for example, said her teaching had been reviewed only twice in her 20-year Andover career. A few chairs who mentioned this inconsistent timing speculated that many delays occurred because the Dean of Faculty's office got behind. (The Dean of Faculty position also rotates every six years, and the lack of an electronic system for the teaching reviews at the school has made it more challenging for the Dean's office to keep track of who had been reviewed in what year.) At the same time, these chairs noted that a more frequent review process would not be realistic.

Second, chairs reported that the expectations and stakes of the formal review were not clear. Some chairs said that the formal review was high-stakes and had implications for salary and continued employment, whereas others characterized the formal review as a developmental conversation intended to help teachers grow their teaching practice. As one chair said, "it [the formal review] is useful that it's oriented around growth, but it's also a performance review." Some chairs, including the chairs who self-identified as people of color, said that the lack of clear expectations made the review process anxiety-inducing and observed that clear expectations—ideally in the form of a definition of good teaching—would be a welcome support for chairs and the faculty under review. At the same time, some chairs worried that articulating clear expectations for teaching would infringe upon faculty autonomy. One chair who self-described as a person of color said,

> Autonomy is wonderful, [faculty of color] can teach what they want to teach in a white male world. On the other hand, it inhibits transparency—certain faculty are worried that leaders will see what they are doing and not like it. Not sure there's a clear answer. I don't want to give up the autonomy to have more transparency. Clear expectations would help; if you know you are doing these things you can rest easy. I do think these guides need to be individual by department because the disciplines are so different.

Most of the chairs we interviewed thought the formal teaching review was useful, or else somewhere between a compliance activity and a useful exercise. None of the chairs with whom we spoke said that the process was without any value. Consistent with the written priorities of the formal review, chairs said that the observations and conversations with the department chair—which afforded an opportunity to talk with peers about instruction—and the written statement—which provided an opportunity to self-reflect—were the most useful pieces of the process. The other parts of teaching review, particularly the summative meeting with the Dean of Faculty and Dean of Studies, felt more compliance-oriented to chairs.

Several chairs suggested that allowing faculty (including chairs, observers, and faculty under review) to dedicate more time to the process would be beneficial. Although none of the chairs with whom we spoke offered specific suggestions for how to dedicate more time, they noted the need for supports to reduce delays in inputs (and in the duration of the review overall), allow flexibility in scheduling observations, and make space for post-observation feedback. In this context, several chairs desired a more sustainable, predictable process. In addition, several chairs recommended that Andover leaders clarify the expectations of the system—whether it is about accountability or feedback—and develop clear expectations for teaching practice.

According to administrators, Andover does not offer formal training for department chairs, peer observers, or the teachers who are being reviewed about the formal evaluation process. The Evaluation Committee members jointly read some texts on instructional coaching, but they do not otherwise receive formal training, although new evaluation committee members may receive some informal training from more experienced colleagues on the committee.

Detail About the Informal, Annual Teaching Reviews

Written Policy

According to Andover's *Faculty Evaluation Handbook*, all teaching faculty are expected to participate in an informal annual evaluation during years when they are not engaged in the periodic formal review. Both the annual informal and periodic formal reviews assess teaching faculty on four dimensions of teaching practice, excerpted from the handbook:

1. Expertise, defined as knowledge of course content and field of study
2. Planning, defined as instructional preparation
3. Implementation, defined as pedagogy, or the methods and practices of teaching, including presentation of content, classroom management, the level of challenge of the content, engagement in teaching and engagement of students in learning, assessment of student learning, and homework
4. Community expectation, or professional conduct, defined as constructive collaboration with colleagues within and across departments and completion of school-wide requirements and obligations, such as attending faculty meetings, keeping class attendance, meeting deadlines for grading.

In informal review years, the *Faculty Evaluation Handbook* stipulates that faculty should set a developmental goal to work on during the next school year, administer the Andover-wide student feedback survey in the last two weeks of the term, and meet with their department or division[6] chair to discuss their developmental goal, their overall performance during the past year, and their professional learning activities for the upcoming year. During this meeting, the faculty member and the chair are expected to complete Andover's

---

[6] Small departments with one or two faculty members (e.g., natural sciences, world languages) are organized into divisions. For example, the natural sciences division includes the physics, biology, and chemistry departments.

Annual Performance Review Form, which is included in the *Faculty Evaluation Handbook*, to document developmental goals and professional learning activities.

Starting in the fourth year of teaching at Andover (i.e., after a first formal review), faculty members are to select one or more professional development activities per year from a menu of options listed on the Annual Performance Review Form. This menu includes doing a peer observation, capturing a video of one's teaching and reflecting on the video, participating in a group of faculty to discuss pedagogy, participating in a conference or workshop, and creating and teaching a new course. The handbook does not specify who will monitor this or how the activities are to be documented.

Practice

Of the 28 chairs of academic departments that we interviewed, only one indicated they followed the written policy for annual reviews.[7] The rest of the chairs we interviewed either told us they had not heard of the annual review or that they were somewhat aware of it, but did not do it. Only one said they had received some training about the annual informal review. A chair who had heard of it but did not do it said, "We were told to prepare people for it, but not to do it. Then we didn't hear much about it for a while. It seemed haphazard and not well coached." A few chairs said that, while they had heard of the process, it was not something that Andover leaders mentioned regularly, and they did not realize it was obligatory. Most chairs said there was no electronic system for tracking these conversations when they did occur, nor was their guidance about what to discuss beyond the form itself, which chairs did not use.

However, about one-third of chairs stated that they had informal annual check-ins with at least some of their faculty. These informal check-in meetings varied. For example, two chairs decided to meet one-on-one with faculty members to ask informally about what things had been difficult during the pandemic and how things were going. A third chair, whose department had fewer than five teaching faculty, said that annually he would review and synthesize the feedback each of his faculty members received on the annual, anonymous student surveys (individual faculty also have access to their survey results). He sent his synthesis in an email to the individual faculty person because that was what his former chair did, and he modelled his practice on that experience. But he did not see how it would be possible to take the time to provide that kind of a written synthesis for each faculty member if he were leading a large department. A fourth chair asked in department faculty meetings at the beginning of the year that each faculty member write down an individual goal for the year and put in an envelope that the faculty member would then open in January. Two additional chairs told us they observed each faculty member in their department teach one class each year. One of these chairs said of this practice, "I think that's something that should happen, but not sure it's an expectation." Some chairs described how they would focus their attention on supporting new teachers in the department. For example, one chair visited new instructors in their classrooms and later discussed the observation and provided feedback.

Chairs in smaller departments expressed the opinion that annual reviews for experienced teachers were unnecessary because faculty frequently had informal interactions in which they discussed teaching and learning. One chair said that because their department was small, "Faculty constantly talk to each other. They have lunch often. They don't have department meetings." Chairs of large departments said that conducting annual reviews of every faculty member would be incredibly time-consuming. For example, one chair of a large department said that when the annual reviews were discussed in academic council, some department chairs "just threw up their hands, [saying] 'This is too much; I can't do it.'" Another chair said

---

[7] A second chair had, before he was a chair, experienced the annual review as described in the *Faculty Evaluation Handbook*, but he did not implement the process once he became a chair.

that the annual reviews "[don't] sound like much, but with everything else we do as chair and as teacher, it's a lot of work."

Despite these concerns, most of the chairs we interviewed said that they found periodic discussions about teaching and learning and professional goals to be an important part of their professional practice. Some of these chairs felt that the conversations did not have to be formal or structured, whereas others thought that some guidelines for the conversation would be helpful. As one chair put it, "I do think that talking to people about what they are working on and being part of the PD [professional development] of people in the department is something I think is really important." Another chair said, "Most people are thinking about their teaching a lot, but not in a formal way."

Detail About the School-Wide Student Survey

Written Policy

Each November, faculty are to administer the school-wide survey in each of their academic classes. The survey was designed by the Faculty Evaluation Committee in 2015, and it is intended to be one measure of teaching practice. Therefore, the survey asks questions that elicit student perceptions about, for example, presentation of content, classroom management, the level of challenge of the content, engagement in teaching and engagement of students in learning, assessment of student learning, and homework.

Survey results are provided to the relevant faculty person and to their department chair, who is expected to summarize the feedback for each faculty member and discuss this summary in their annual informal and periodic formal teaching reviews. The written materials we reviewed did not provide any guidance for how department chairs (or faculty) should analyze or summarize student survey responses.

The 2015 Faculty Evaluation Committee report recommended development and use of a script that faculty could opt to read to students prior to administering the survey. The purpose of such a script would be to help students offer constructive feedback to faculty.

Practice

Almost all faculty administer the anonymous student survey annually according to department chairs, but faculty do not find the results useful for their practice. Most chairs told us that many faculty believed the results to be biased or otherwise unhelpful for improving their instruction, and use of the data was low. All chairs said that they believed student feedback to be an important source of feedback about their instruction, but that they preferred surveys developed by their departments or themselves as a more useful source. Chair comments highlighted the tension inherent in using the school-wide survey for both a developmental and a managerial purpose; almost all chairs reported that the survey served neither purpose well.

All but one of the chairs we interviewed said that all or almost all teachers in their department administered the survey in class during the last two weeks of the fall term, prior to calculating final grades, and that all students in attendance generally took the survey.[8] Chairs reported that they received the results after final grades were in. A few chairs mentioned that there was room for departments to add their own questions to the school-wide survey.

Although the 2015 Faculty Evaluation Committee report mentioned a script that faculty could use to prepare students to provide thoughtful feedback, none of the chairs we interviewed said that they were provided

---

[8] The one chair who had not administered it yet was new to the position in fall 2021 and our interviews occurred before the survey administration window.

with such a script. About a third of the chairs said such a script would be useful. Nevertheless, most chairs used their own introductory language when administering the survey. Chairs said that, when they administered the student survey in their own classes, they reminded students that the survey was anonymous, that their feedback was important, that students should be honest and thoughtful, and that they would not get in trouble for providing honest comments. A few said they mentioned to students that the results were used to evaluate the faculty members and would be seen by the department chair. As one chair said, "I have a script, but it wasn't given to me. It was something I developed. I ask kids to be candid to help me as a teacher and improve the class."

Most chairs said that they looked at the results—and thought most of the faculty in their departments looked at them too—but few chairs said they produced a written summary of results for each faculty person as suggested by the written policy. Only six chairs said they discussed the survey results with faculty regardless of the results; most chairs said they discussed the results only if there was an issue or concern. Only one chair reported receiving guidance from Andover leaders about how to interpret and use the survey results; most chairs had not received such guidance, but said that they would welcome it.

When describing their own approaches to interpreting the survey results, most chairs said that they scanned the Likert scale items for patterns and read through the written comments with an eye toward any specific concerns. All chairs who discussed their approach to analysis said they tended to ignore negative outlier responses. One chair described their process this way:

> I did look at the results for all my faculty, but in a diagnostic way for issues that needed addressing. It was managerial reading, quality control, looking for fires to put out, looking at the Likert items and comments. There's an editorial sense you get when reading and can quickly see if one student is being negative, that doesn't warrant attention as chair.

A few chairs noted that the survey interface (Qualtrics) was cumbersome and that analyzing results for faculty in their department—especially for open-ended responses—was time-consuming.

Chair perceptions of whether the survey accurately captured teaching quality varied. Roughly a third viewed it as a pro forma exercise, roughly a third found the survey results helpful and accurate, and the final third expressed mixed views or said the accuracy of the feedback depended on the student. In general, chairs who viewed the survey as a pro forma exercise and those who held mixed views expressed strong concerns that student feedback about teaching quality is inherently biased. Concerns about bias reflect two themes consistent with the literature (as we discuss in Chapter 4): concern that students are not able to be objective and that they can be biased against faculty who are female and/or people of color.

Chairs who expressed concerns about student objectivity worried that the results are a "popularity contest" and reflect how well a student likes a teacher; that students use the survey to "get back" at faculty for things such as poor grades; that students do not know what good teaching is; that responses reflect enjoyment of the class rather than learning; and responses reflect the student's mood that day. One chair said, "It's more about how much the student likes you and your teaching than it is about teaching quality." Another commented that "Easy graders are rewarded on the survey." Another chair said, "It feels personal. [It] feels like punishment for the teacher."

Chairs raised concerns about bias based on identity characteristics and said that faculty who identified as female and/or people of color received systematically lower responses than their male and/or white peers and that students raised more concerns about their qualifications and teaching. One chair who expressed this concern said, "It's a bad tool that's used against teachers, especially faculty of color. Science has proved over and over how easy it is to pick on faculty of color." Another said that faculty of color are "second-guessed" more often and that it takes longer to earn the respect of students, peers, and parents: "It [respect] comes, but it doesn't come easily."

One chair said that teaching students how to provide constructive feedback was not an emphasis at Andover and that a script, while helpful, would not be enough. This person implied that spending more time teaching students how to give constructive feedback could mitigate some faculty members' concerns about bias. In their words: "We don't do a good job at this school of instructing students in how to give feedback. I think we need to go beyond a script, need to practice with students how to give constructive feedback."

Some chairs who held negative or mixed views of the survey explained that while students could be objective with their responses, the information in the survey is generic and unhelpful for improving their instruction. One chair said, "I think the surveys are valid—students don't lie —but the data aren't that useful." A few chairs noted that department or course-specific surveys would mitigate this concern. As one person said, "We cannot get meaningful feedback if every department is using the same form." As a result, noted another chair, "I think most people look [at the survey], but may not do much with it."

About half of chairs said that many of their concerns about the survey stemmed from the lack of clear guidance about how the results should be interpreted and used. Although most chairs we interviewed said they did not use the data in this way, chairs who expressed this concern were particularly worried that negative outlier responses would affect their salary or continued employment at Andover and perceived that faculty who identify as female and/or people of color were particularly vulnerable to negative consequences. Broadly, these comments reflect chairs' perception that the purpose of the survey—developmental or managerial—is unclear. As one chair said,

> There are lots of binary questions about what is going on in the class which can be useful to the chair to catch problems, especially for new teachers. But if the goal is developmental for the teacher, for example, how do we help teachers who are doing a good job get better? That's a different survey with different questions.

Despite these concerns, all chairs endorsed the idea that student feedback is important and can be useful for improving instruction. Most chairs said they or their colleagues sought student feedback using surveys they designed themselves or had been designed collaboratively within the department. (Ninety-three percent of faculty who participated in our winter 2022 questionnaire indicated they had administered one or more student surveys for their own purposes at Andover. We describe the faculty questionnaires in Chapter 4.) Chairs reported administering brief surveys in Canvas, Google Forms, or Microsoft Forms. The content of the surveys focused on eliciting student preferences and study habits, reactions to course assignments or content, and suggestions for improving the course. Example questions included "Are we meeting your needs?" "What are your goals for this class?" "What work are you most proud of?" As one chair said, "In my survey, I want to know things about what the kids prefer, e.g., many small quizzes over one test, or learn the grammar at home and practice in class—nuts and bolts pedagogy." In general, chairs who used these self-administered surveys often administered them mid-term so that they could use the information to improve the course in the second half of the term. Several chairs noted that an advantage of self- or department-developed surveys is that (as one chair said) "the kids are talking to me." In contrast, when taking the school-wide survey, students are talking to someone "above" the instructor, which could influence the content and depth of students' comments.

Andover's Departmental Review Processes

Andover does not have written expectations for departmental operations or departmental reviews. In the absence of a written description, we instead describe the variety of actions and practices individual department chairs[9] told us they use to reflect on, update, or improve the content they teach and their goals for teaching. Activities could include reviewing curriculum, aligning curriculum content across sections of a course and throughout a series of courses (i.e., from the 100 to 400 level), or developing or revising student learning goals (also known as *competencies*).

Overall, chairs described departmental review processes that were organic, informal, and chair-driven. One chair said, "Department evaluations need to happen. It's useful for each department to create their own way of doing it, based on teaching methodology and style." All the chairs who spoke about departmental reviews expressed that they were interested in continuously improving course content and teaching, and in ensuring that that the discipline is accessible to students at all levels of interest and aptitude. As one chair said, "It's an incremental, evolving process we get to as we can. We tackle little pieces each year, which works well; we don't have capacity to do more. This approach allows us to test things and adjust." For example, one chair explained that faculty within the department adjusted course content to make entry-level courses more accessible to students without prior knowledge of the field.

Review activities differed by department, but there was broad agreement that such activities were helpful. There was also broad agreement on the types of activities that were appropriate for a departmental review. Such activities included aligning curriculum content across sections of a course and throughout a series of courses, laying out what students should be able to know and do and when, and grade norming and equity in grading. A few chairs said they brought in outside observers from other schools or outside consultants to assist with these activities. One chair said, "we have been working on horizontal and vertical coordination for a long time, and looking at creating standards to ensure faculty are using similar grading criteria and teaching aligned content across 100-200-300 courses."

The timing and duration of these activities also varied by department and division. Sometimes a curriculum review was sparked by a specific event, such as the selection of an incoming chair or the hiring of several new faculty members as others retired. More often, though, chairs said that their department took an incremental approach because finding the time to dedicate to this work was challenging. A few chairs said that they used the two planning days (known as "division days") for department review activities, but that otherwise finding time during the academic year was difficult. A few chairs said that they had participated in department-wide review activities during the summer, but that timing was challenging because of vacation plans. A few faculty members said they applied for Tang Institute grants for course relief, which allowed them to engage in developing new courses or examining grading during the academic year. As one chair said, "We don't want people to work on [curriculum review] without getting paid; the work has to be manageable, but that's hard to carve out."

Two chairs suggested that some departmental review activity should be part of the chair's responsibilities during their six-year term, and that classroom observations could be a useful activity to support within-department alignment. One of these chairs said, "I think it would help to have a department review process just to affirm what we are doing. It could be every six years to coincide with the term of a chair, and the chair would set an agenda for their tenure. The mandate would be to do it, not to implement what the chair says."

---

[9] All but three chairs described how their departments or divisions approach departmental review and we heard from at least one chair in each division and department.

CHAPTER 3

The Research About Teaching and Departmental Reviews as Applied to Independent Schools

To develop recommendations for Andover, we first reviewed published research about three topics—evaluations of teaching practice, instructor professional learning, and departmental reviews—for three separate categories of U.S. schools: independent high schools, four-year colleges and universities, and public kindergarten through 12th grade (K–12) schools. Because of the paucity of published research about independent schools, we looked to the much larger body of research about K–12 public school settings and from postsecondary schools. Yet there are significant differences between these and independent school settings.

Therefore, we also interviewed administrators at eight independent schools across the United States and representatives from four networks of independent schools.[1] One interviewee at an independent school association told us that well-executed teaching review systems in independent schools are the exception rather than the norm, as reviewing teaching well is "hard work." To help Andover and other independent schools with their own planning, we provide concrete examples of how these schools enacted their policies wherever relevant throughout the chapter.

We did not ask independent schools about every activity we describe below (e.g., peer observations and grade norming), so some sections of this chapter only summarize published research. To fill some remaining gaps in the K–16 education research, we also consulted literature from other sectors such as health care and public-sector performance management systems in a few instances that we note below. We detail our literature review and interview methods in Appendix A.

Key Takeaways

- Andover's evaluations of teaching practice, instructor professional learning, and departmental reviews should be part of a larger, coherent instructional system.
- A coherent instructional system starts with identifying the skills and knowledge that the school's instruction should impart to students, then ensures that curricula cover these skills and knowledge as do classroom assessments, and ends with both professional learning for teachers and a teaching review system that aligns with those desired skills and knowledge.
- Departments can be the engine to create a coherent instructional system.
- Student surveys are extremely helpful for low-stakes, developmental use, and they should be carefully designed when used for high-stakes purposes. Research identifies ways to reduce biases in their responses.

---

[1] Broadly speaking, these four organizations—the National Association of Independent Schools, Folio, Mastery Collaborative, and 1SchoolHouse—provide services (e.g., technology platforms, professional development) and resources (e.g., examples of observation tools or teacher/student competencies) to help independent schools design and implement processes for reviewing teaching practice.

- A teaching review system needs to be simple enough to be sustained over time, and faculty should be trained about how to execute it. Teacher buy-in and institutional commitment are key to a successful teaching review system.

What's the Goal? Schools Should Have Coherent Instructional Systems to Promote Consistent Student Academic Experiences

A well-designed instructional system should ensure that students and teachers have consistent instruction that, over the course of four years, instills the desired skills and knowledge Andover wishes students to learn. We use Newmann et al.'s definition of instructional program coherence: "a set of interrelated programs for students and staff that are guided by a common framework for curriculum, instruction, assessment, and learning climate and are pursued over a sustained period" (Newmann et al., 2001).

The key components of a coherent instructional system are as follows:

1. a clear identification of student skills and knowledge (i.e., competencies) that curricula should cover,
2. use of curricula that covers the desired competencies
3. teachers' use of assessments that are aligned to the curriculum
4. professional learning for teachers that covers the curriculum and the desired student skills and knowledge
5. a teaching review that gauges whether teachers use the common instructional framework (i.e., desired student skills and knowledge and teacher competencies) in their courses.

Put another way, a coherent instructional system would ensure that courses of study, instructional materials (including lesson plans, syllabi, and digital materials), professional learning opportunities, student assessments (including grading rubrics), and teaching reviews would all be aligned to a common set of desired teacher and student competencies or skills and to each other (Polikoff et al., 2020; Newmann et al., 2001). Achieving coherence is an ongoing process; if one component changes, others should similarly adjust.

Academic Departments as the Engine of a Coherent Instructional System

In this section, we review literature and summarize independent school interviews about the role academic departments can play in designing and enacting several elements of a coherent instructional system. We are not aware of empirical research that demonstrates an inherent advantage to either a department-centric or a centralized approach to designing and maintaining a coherent instructional system. But we chose in this section to summarize research and interviews about a department-centric approach for the following three reasons:

- Andover faculty's strong preference (discussed in Chapter 4) for a departmental rather than centralized approach
- research evidence about the importance of faculty buy-in
- the ubiquity of a department-centric approach (balanced with guidance and support from the central administration) at the independent schools where we interviewed.

As we describe in the following sub-sections, departments can develop department-specific definitions of: student competencies and teacher competencies, and an instructional map of their courses. To ensure that students receive a coherent course of instruction school-wide, a central committee can then work with the departments to ensure some degree of continuity. Departments can then revisit their specific versions on an ongoing basis to ensure that they support a coherent instructional system through curriculum mapping, grade norming, and student assessment studies. With a culture of continuous improvement, departments can self-select topics for study each year and enlist external observers on a periodic basis.

Most of the literature we identified about specific departmental review activities comes from postsecondary rather than K–12 settings, and we draw on the K–12 literature in specific instances. We also draw on interviews we conducted of independent school leaders. In general, the specific activities mentioned by our eight school administrator interviewees mirrored those used in postsecondary institutions.

Identify Student and Then Teacher Competencies

Student competencies are the essential skills, knowledge, habits of mind, and behaviors that students are expected to master before they graduate. They are the spine of an instructional framework, from which desired teaching competencies, coursework, student assessment, and teacher development flow (Kalu and Dyjur, 2018; Lindholm, 2009). Put another way, student competencies form an actionable "commitment" that enable students to fulfill a school's "vision for learning" (Hudson, 2019).

While the terms used for student competencies vary in the literature and in our independent school interviews (e.g., program learning outcomes, student learning outcomes, standards, profile of a graduate), the concepts are similar. The idea is to break broader program and institutional goals for student learning into smaller, measurable components (Lindholm, 2009).

In the United States, all seven major regional accreditors require colleges and universities to specify program learning outcomes and use these to drive institutional improvement, which has in turn increased their adoption in higher education (Andrade, 2018; Provezis, 2010). In a 2017 national survey of leaders from regionally accredited postsecondary institutions, 82 percent reported adoption of an explicit set of student learning outcomes common to all majors, and 50 percent said that each individual department had program-specific outcomes that aligned with broader institutional goals for student learning (Jankowski et al., 2018). NEASC has encouraged Andover to adopt student competencies, using the term *profile of a graduate.*

To ensure that student competencies are actionable and clear, they should be written using the same structures and syntax as program learning outcomes, which are more substantiated in the literature (Kennedy, Hyland, and Ryan, 2009; Adelman, 2015; Kennedy, 2006; Schoepp, 2019). Student competencies, like program learning outcomes, should consist of three parts: (1) a student-centered introductory stem, (2) concrete or operational verbs, and (3) a focus on demonstrable skills and knowledge (Adelman, 2015; Kennedy, 2006; Schoepp, 2019). Beyond this, the following set of norms has emerged from the numerous guidance documents directed toward postsecondary instructions issued by accreditation agencies, postsecondary institutions, and pedagogical experts, and from our independent school interviews:

- Make it a team effort. The independent schools we interviewed engaged faculty in the development and revision of student competencies. High levels of participation will support a shared understanding of institutional and departmental priorities for student learning (Kalu and Dyjur, 2018; Provezis, 2010; Dyjur and Lock, 2016).
- Be consistent. Student competencies should be based on institutional and departmental goals for learning, which themselves are derived from a formalized understanding of institutional mission and purpose, a practice adopted in the independent schools we interviewed. Faculty and staff should, for example, consult foundational documents (i.e., mission statements, strategic planning documents, program-specific descriptions), examine relevant educational literature, survey alumni about their

experiences, and collect information from peer organizations (Chance and Peck, 2015; Dyjur and Kalu, 2016; Kalu and Dyjur, 2018; Lindholm, 2009).

- Choose what matters most. The literature we found, as well as our interviews with independent school administrators, suggests that departments should choose "a manageable number of competencies," which translates to roughly from four to ten (Chance and Peck, 2015; Kennedy, 2006). These choices should be based on the most important academic goals for students in each department and framed in terms of what students should know and be able to do before they graduate. They should neither be too broad nor too specific (Lindholm, 2009; Schoepp, 2019).
- Select only observable competencies. There are four types of competencies: knowledge, skills, attitudes and values, and behavior (Lindholm, 2009). No type is more important than the others; however, they do not equally lend themselves to measurement. During the development phase, it is important to consider whether competencies are observable (i.e., is it possible to directly or indirectly observe whether students have achieved a desired objective). While older sources suggest that learning outcomes may be "aspirational" rather than directly observable, more recent literature suggests that effective program learning outcomes are both observable and measurable (Chance and Peck, 2015).
- Attend to syntax. Choose verbs that are measurable and imply observable, concrete student activities (create, apply, interpret, describe, identify, categorize) and avoid excessive wordiness. A popular source for inspiration is the taxonomy first developed by Benjamin Bloom in 1956 and then revised in 2001 (Armstrong, 2010; Schoepp, 2019; Chance and Peck, 2015; Adelman, 2015; Kennedy, 2006).
- Make them public. Student competencies communicate to current and prospective students and their parents what is expected of them and what is valuable about the institution and each academic program. Knowing what is expected may improve student efficacy and support decisionmaking about course selection (Lindholm, 2009).

The eight independent schools we interviewed were all in the process of developing school-wide goals for student learning and a common instructional vision. To provide Andover with concrete examples, we describe here the two schools (The Dalton School and Holton-Arms School) with the most detailed explanations about their processes.

Dalton started what its leaders expect will be a five to seven-year process to create a coherent instructional system by first developing student (and teacher, as we describe later in this section) competencies. Dalton's departments started by writing a department-specific mission statement that was consistent with the overall school mission and then developed specific student competencies aligned to that mission. Dalton plans to incorporate the department-developed student competencies into a set of school-wide goals for student learning, using the term *profile of a graduate*. The student competencies have enabled observers and teachers to have clear conversations about how well the lesson was aligned to the department mission and goals for student learning.

Holton-Arms started with a school-wide process, drawing on the feedback that came out of its most recent self-study wherein they asked the question "what do we value, and what's important for students at the end of the day?" Holton-Arms identified three institutional priorities around which it built student competencies: diversity, equity, and inclusion; global competency; and wellness and social and emotional skills, which include physical and mental health. Holton-Arms looked to outside sources (e.g., the Asia Society for global competencies, CASEL [Collaborative for Academic, Social, and Emotional Learning] for social and emotional learning competences) for inspiration, and developed eight school-wide goals, each with eight to ten competencies. Departments then mimicked the school-wide process, creating their own goals and competencies. Holton-Arms began its five-year process by developing a curriculum review process. It then developed school-wide student competencies in the second year and departmental student competencies in the third year.

Teaching competencies should be aligned to student competencies and to the school's instructional vision. Most of the research we identified about written teacher competencies comes from the public K–12 literature. K–12 public school systems typically rely on standard tools, such as the Danielson Framework for Teaching or the Classroom Assessment Scoring System (CLASS) to define the competencies for which its teachers are accountable (Close, Amrein-Beardsley, and Collins, 2020). In general, these "off the shelf" instruments measure observable teaching behaviors in the classroom (Joe et al., 2013); although they do not have to be limited to just classroom activity. Depending on a school's underlying philosophy of teaching and learning (e.g., constructivism, emphasis on teacher-student relationships), different instruments measure different aspects of teaching, including such constructs as planning and preparation, classroom management, and content knowledge (Gill et al., 2016). We revisit these instruments in more detail below when we discuss classroom observations later in this chapter.

The independent school administrators we interviewed took different approaches to developing teaching competencies—some developed teacher competencies first, and then developed student competencies; others developed student competencies first; and others developed both in parallel. All eight schools operationalized their common instructional vision by developing a school-wide definition of good teaching practices (most schools called this definition "teacher competencies") that faculty across departments should strive to reflect in their practice. We describe four schools below.

For example, Dalton is developing a teacher observation tool, or rubric, that outlines a teachers' professional responsibilities based on Dalton's agreed upon teaching competencies. Dalton initially considered using a commercial tool, such as the Danielson Framework for Teaching, which is commonly used in public schools, but ultimately abandoned it because the school deemed it too complicated and time-consuming to use. Like other schools, Dalton relied on available frameworks for examples of how to structure teaching competencies, and what language to use, to develop its own competencies.

Mercersburg Academy has convened two school-wide committees to develop teacher competencies in parallel with its student competencies. These committees are chaired by faculty members and include school administrators. A smaller group of faculty and administrators from both committees works to ensure alignment across these parallel efforts. Mercersburg, like Andover and several other independent schools we interviewed, is a member of Mastery Collaborative, and has drawn on its materials and examples for guidance. Other schools, such as Holton-Arms and Pomfret School, are working with Folio, another consortium of independent schools, to develop teacher competencies. Like the Mastery Collaborative schools, they are drawing on Folio's experience and examples (we also interviewed staff from Folio), as well as its data management system, to develop teacher competencies that are aligned to student competencies and the school mission.

Curriculum Mapping Is a Key Exercise to Build Instructional Coherence

A curriculum map is a visualization of what is being taught in each department at each grade, with the map outlining the relationships within and between the courses in a program of study (Greatorex et al., 2019; Kalu and Dyjur, 2018). An aligned curriculum means that at each stage, students will accumulate knowledge and skills that build on past learning and lay the foundation for future coursework. A map is intended to ensure that, over the progression of their program of study, students will acquire the full set of desired competencies (Rawle et al., 2017; Schutte, Line, and McCullick, 2018). The actual mapping can be done in a spreadsheet or through another sequence mapping tool. While maps can take a variety of forms, a typical structure, adapted from Schutte, Line, and McCullick (2018), consists of Institutional Learning Goals or Competencies → Departmental or Program Student Competencies → Course Competencies or Objectives.

In postsecondary institutions, curriculum mapping is a useful tool for engaging faculty in conversations about the scope and sequence of student learning, creating program coherence, and increasing curricular transparency (Harden, 2001; Kalu and Dyjur, 2018). Put another way, the process of curriculum mapping—as well as the finished map itself—can be a productive way for faculty to talk about how their courses build toward the knowledge and skills students are expected to acquire (Kopera-Frye, Mahaffy, and Svare, 2008; Bester and Scholtz, 2012). Academic departments can also use curriculum maps to coordinate classroom activities, structure scaffolding, plan program evaluation, inform teaching reviews, and build teams (Schutte, Line, and McCullick, 2019).

The process of curriculum mapping can be challenging, however. Difficulties that may arise among faculty include different conceptualizations of key terminology, philosophical differences, and trouble discerning between inter-related competencies (Ervin, Carter, and Robinson, 2013). Another challenge is identifying the degree to which a particular course helps students meet a given competency—for example, an upper-level course should provide deeper understanding and more thorough exposure, practice, and repeated application of a concept than a lower-level course. Other issues include faculty time (i.e., curriculum mapping may require considerable time resources), "idea negotiation" when faculty are not able to reach a consensus, and training new staff members (Jacobsen et al., 2018). There is no clear consensus in the literature for addressing these challenges; however, Jacobsen et al. talk about the importance of clearly documenting all decisionmaking to ensure that "issues get revisited regularly and discussed with subsequent design teams," including new members of the team.

Although there are many possible approaches to curriculum mapping, we summarize Uchiyama, Pippin, and Radin's (2009) six-step process designed to foster collaboration among faculty members:

1. Each instructor individually maps the objectives from their current courses, making sure their course objects align with department-level student competencies. Mapping can happen in real time (as a course unfolds over the semester) or instructors can work from their own syllabi.
2. Instructors of identical courses work together to aggregate their maps. In doing so, they begin to create an aligned vision of what their course should entail.
3. At the department level, all faculty review the maps for their respective program or sequence of courses to identify gaps, overlap, and strengths.
4. At the department level, faculty collaborate to ensure coherence in each program of study by bringing each course into alignment with one another and department-level student competencies.
5. Faculty make requisite changes to their courses to bring them into alignment.
6. The process is repeated as often as deemed necessary.

In our interviews of independent schools, four explained their curriculum mapping process. For example, at Holton-Arms departments are expected to develop individual courses and courses of study that are aligned to the school-wide instructional vision and teacher and student competencies. Then, instructors who teach the same course work off the same curriculum map to ensure that students in different sections of a course will have a reasonably consistent experience. At Pomfret, curriculum mapping draws on school-wide resources, such as standards for how a typical syllabus should look and guidelines for how class time should be used. Washington International School used a similar process as Pomfret, and both schools were early in the development process.

Peer Reviews of Teaching Can Help Create a Collaborative Environment Around Instruction

Collaborative peer review involves teachers observing other teachers' practices and learning through the exchange of productive feedback. This is the same model Andover faculty endorsed, in the first round of their feedback (see Chapter 4 for more details), as part of departmental self-studies. Compared with other sources of feedback, peer review is a popular choice for teachers. In a 2017 nationally representative survey of teachers, 86 percent rated informal feedback from peers as helpful, compared with 74 percent about informal feedback from school leaders (Prado Tuma, Hamilton, and Tsai, 2018). At its best, teacher participation in a no-stakes peer review can lead to deeper self-reflection into one's own practice, shared awareness among staff of students' learning experiences, institutionally coherent practices, and increased levels of teacher confidence (Bell and Thomson, 2018).

Collaborative peer review can serve multiple purposes, such as evidence gathering for departmental self-study, professional learning, or lesson study. Regardless of its purpose, collaborative peer review should be as simple, straightforward, and consistent as possible. Like any professional learning activity, one of the most commonly identified barriers to successful implementation of peer review throughout the K–12 and postsecondary literature is lack of time (Timperley, 2015). Therefore, it is important that teachers spend the time they do have engaging in meaningful dialogue with colleagues rather than completing compliance activities.

Many postsecondary and K–12 sources recommend a three-step model for effective peer review. Drawing on established best practices (Bell and Cooper, 2013; Whitlock and Rumpus, 2004; Sachs and Parsell, 2013; Martin and Double, 1998) and firsthand experience in a large academic department, Fletcher (2018) describes the three-step model that Andover already largely follows: a pre-meeting, followed by an observation, followed by a post-observation feedback conversation.

The success of peer review depends on the extent to which participants are mutually committed to reaching understanding about their practices rather than making judgements (Gosling, 2002). If teachers are not fully bought in or think the peer review might influence their own formal evaluations, they might choose to share samples of their instruction that are not representative of their typical lessons or fail to provide constructive feedback (Hammersley-Fletcher and Orsmond, 2004). These are concerns that some Andover department chairs raised in our interviews. Keeping the peer observations expressly separate from teachers' formal evaluations can help maintain the openness and trust needed for productive peer review.

Even with a peer review process that is purely for formative purpose and that is not tied to a teacher's formal evaluation by the school, it is still important to put structures in place to minimize possible sources of observer bias (e.g., the nature of the relationship between observer and observed, intimidation, and implicit sources of bias based on race or gender). Please see "Teaching Evaluation Systems as a Part of a Larger, Coherent Instructional System" below for a more thorough discussion of specific types of bias that might surface in the peer review process and suggestions for reducing bias during observations.

Grade Norming Helps to Ensure Students Receive Consistent Feedback About Their Work

The 2022 Andover Anti-Racist Taskforce report and the NAESC report to Andover each noted that students do not always have consistent experiences, and they urged Andover to strive for greater consistency while also preserving valued faculty autonomy. One way departments could improve consistency of student experiences is by examining variation in the grading of student work.

Such variation—on both low- and high-stakes assignments—has implications for students' academic futures (O'Connell et al., 2016). This variation risks inequitable outcomes, not least because teachers tend to grade certain groups more favorably than others. Numerous studies highlight that differential grading linked to student characteristics (e.g., race and gender) is prevalent in schools around the world (Hanna and Linden, 2012; Hinnerich, Höglin, and Johannesson, 2011). For instance, one study of high school students across North Carolina indicated that teachers overall graded female students higher and low-income students lower relative to standardized measures of learning (Rauschenberg, 2014). These biases are often unintentional and can be mitigated.

One way to limit differential grading is via grade norming, or calibrating grading practices across teachers and classrooms (Malouff, 2008). Norming is a multistep "collaborative process that requires discussion leading to evidence-driven consensus—a procedure where examples from student work are used to justify scores leading to a shared understanding amongst raters" (Schoepp, Danaher, and Ater Kranov, 2018). Grade norming is a common departmental review activity at the postsecondary level and was used by a few of the independent schools we interviewed.

The research on grade norming is surprisingly slim. There is much more research on developing assessments, assignments, and rubrics than there is on the ways that teachers calibrate their grading with one another. We draw from the available literature in K–12 and postsecondary settings and from literature regarding other processes of teacher consensus-building, such as collaborative inquiry intended to improve teachers' practice *through* looking at student work, and the conditions that support or hinder their success.

Research suggests several factors promote effective grade norming. It is important for teachers to meet regularly, negotiate ground rules for their collaborative work, and set timelines (Langer, Colton, and Goff, 2003). Teacher teams should use a protocol to focus their norming processes (Flowers, Mertens, and Mulhall, 2005).[2] Different protocols prioritize different activities, prompts, and foci (Levine and Marcus, 2010), so schools should select a protocol that aligns with their instructional vision and goals. Almost universally, calibration protocols direct teachers to identify examples of student work that fit different grading criteria (these are often called "anchor" documents) and are used as references when grading additional work. Research indicates that anchor documents play a key role in promoting consistent grading (Hardre, 2014; Wang et al., 2017).

Organizational supports can increase the chance that grade norming will be successful. For instance, teachers' norming will be more fruitful if their school provides a model for teachers to work from (Wayman, Midgley, and Stringfield, 2005). Teachers can benefit from professional development and practice norming (Wang et al., 2017). Finally, a common constraint on all forms of teacher collaboration is the number of other demands on their attention (Nelson et al., 2008); if leadership is to prioritize teachers' norming processes, it may need to substitute other responsibilities (e.g., using time already reserved for staff meetings to instead focus on norming activities).

The Research About External Department Reviews Yields Mixed Results

Independent K–12 schools and postsecondary institutions commonly engage in external reviews, in which visitors from peer institutions meet with faculty to provide an independent view of curricula, teaching materials, and strategies. These low-stakes meetings are intended to be informal exchanges of ideas and information. Although reviews are an intuitively useful approach, we found little literature that describes common processes or describes the nature of the learning, self-reflection, and improvement that can result. We drew on this limited literature in the United States and in international settings.

Departmental review processes can be considered a type of horizontal accountability in the sense that a department is accountable to a peer organization or department that is not in a supervisory role (Schil-

---

[2] There are numerous publicly available protocol options, such as WestEd's Analysis for Student Work Protocol, the Calibration Protocol for Scoring Student Work from the Rhode Island Department of Education, and the Semi-Structured Calibration Activity Protocol from the Stanford Center for Assessment, Learning and Inquiry.

lemans, 2011; Kezar and El-Khawas, 2003). Department reviews range from purely internal departmental reviews (e.g., a chemistry department reviews a math department within the school) to small groups of external visitors, such as one or two invited academics from other institutions to enhanced accreditation processes. These reviews typically result in recommendations to the host institution often conveyed in an internal report (Schillemans, 2011).

Of course, the quality and usefulness of such reviews can vary. For example, there is strong potential for review findings to be biased in favor of the host institution (Silva, Reich, and Gallegos, 1997), reducing their accuracy and value. But when done well, reviews can help programs or departments learn what they need to improve (Trow, 1994; Schillemans, 2011), a process than can result in productive change when the receiving organization has a culture of continuous improvement (Harvey, 1998). Thus, candor and reflectiveness are crucial, and institutions should avoid actions that threaten the trust and openness necessary for internally driven improvements (Newton, 2000; Trow, 1994; Shah, 2012).

Some K–12 schools have an analogous process called *school inspections* or *school quality reviews*. They date back to 1839 in the United Kingdom and have grown into a popular accountability approach globally (Rothman, 2018). These inspections—often referenced as the *Inspectorate model* or *Ofsted inspections* in the UK—bring external educators and trained inspectors to the school for periodic visits that involve self-reflection, data review, classroom observations, and interviews. Despite widespread use, there is little research documenting the effectiveness of school inspection, and what we do know points to mixed results (Ehren et al., 2013; Ehren et al., 2015; Ehren and Visscher, 2008; Hussain, 2015). For example, a five-year study showed mixed results with slightly positive impact on test scores for students in selective state-run schools and slightly negative impact on test scores for students in nonselective state-run schools (Shaw et al., 2003). Other studies have demonstrated some short-term improvements in test scores in low-performing schools, but only temporarily.

Since the 1990s, some public school systems in the United States have adopted a modified version of school inspection, often called School Quality Review. These reviews are intended to provide feedback on instructional quality and opportunities for improvement (Rothman, 2018). A high-quality system can be costly if done regularly and extensively (Jerald, 2012) and requires investment in building capacity and expertise (Berner, 2017).

Teaching Evaluation Systems as a Part of a Larger, Coherent Instructional System

In this section, we summarize the K–12 research and independent school interviews about the traditional elements of a teacher performance review system—classroom observations, student surveys, feedback conversations—and how the system is organized as a whole. Teaching reviews are both a professional development tool and a means to ensure accountability to individual or organizational goals and make staffing decisions (Greenfield et al., 2022; Stecher et al., 2010).

Teaching review systems can be evaluative and high-stakes—as is the case in some K–12 public school systems—or they can be developmental and low-stakes in the sense that they do not determine employment decisions and pay, as is the case at the independent schools we interviewed and Andover and most postsecondary institutions (aside from tenure review). Whereas evaluative models are meant to demonstrate progress toward some set of standards, developmental models rely on feedback from educational experts such as department chairs or instructional coaches to improve teacher quality through constructive conversation.

In interviews of independent school leaders and independent schools' service organizations such as Folio, we learned that, in practice, most of the independent schools operated two parallel tracks for teacher evaluation: (1) an annual developmental teaching review process that is intended to promote the professional growth of each teacher, and (2) a narrower, evaluative human resources process to address infrequent instances of underperformance or of mismatch of the teacher with the school.

An alternative is to seek to combine both streams into one system, which public K–12 teacher evaluation systems do (Stecher et al., 2018). However, blending both streams into one necessitates a high degree of standardization of the teaching review process—for example, the use of a validated classroom observation protocol on which observers are trained to meet or exceed thresholds of inter-rater reliability. These K–12 systems have also typically fallen far short of their goal of promoting teacher development, which is arguably the central goal for Andover's redesign of its evaluation (Kraft and Christian, 2021; Hunter and Springer, 2022; Stecher et al., 2018).

The Independent High Schools Included in Our Interviews Ran Their Teaching Reviews Through Departments

Our literature search did not uncover any systematic research about evaluations of teaching in independent schools, so we once again relied on our interviews with eight school administrators and four staff at independent school service organizations. The eight administrators we spoke with said that their schools were all reviewing and revamping their teaching review processes. Like Andover, other schools paused their teaching reviews because of the COVID-19 pandemic. School leaders reported taking the opportunity to reduce the burden of evaluations on faculty and administrators and to align the process with the school's instructional vision as part of the process of building a coherent instructional system.

Although their specific processes and timelines differed, the independent school teaching review systems we learned about shared a common goal: to create a cohesive, consistent learning experience for students across departments and across years/grade levels of study. They used teaching reviews to support coherence by framing them as a means of continuous improvement of instructional practice aligned with the school's teacher and student competencies.

Like public schools, the independent schools engaged in classroom observations and administered student feedback surveys, activities that serve as the basis of developmental conversations about instruction. Unlike public schools, independent schools tend not to quantify classroom observation and student survey results to produce a numeric score for performance management. The independent school administrators and experts we spoke with said they developed their own observation tools and student feedback instruments in alignment with their student and teacher competencies and opted not to use the commercially available tools commonly used in public schools, which were too complex and burdensome to administer. According to one professional association of independent schools, the most common commercially available tool that independent schools use is the Danielson Framework for Teaching, but he said that most then modified and greatly simplified the tool, adding that independent schools tend to want to customize their approach.

Public schools—and, as far as we can tell, a much smaller portion of independent schools—also use instructional coaching, in which trained observers use a common observation tool to take low-inference notes (i.e., notes that do not make assumptions about the reasons for teacher or student actions but instead merely record the action) about teaching practice. Observations are followed by a coaching conversation, in which the observer and teacher discuss the lesson and strategies for continuous improvement. In independent schools and postsecondary institutions, observers are generally department chairs but can also be faculty peers; in public K–12 schools observers are often school principals, designated instructional coaches, or district administrators.

As described by our interviewees, reviews of teaching in independent schools often shared the following characteristics:

- Grounded in a common instructional vision. This vision was codified by a portrait of a graduate that articulates a school-wide vision for the knowledge and skills students should acquire and be able to demonstrate.
- Articulated a school-wide vision of good teaching. The language used to describe this definition varied; some schools called these teaching competences, or best practices.
- Focused on teacher development and on continuous improvement of teaching practice rather than management or accountability. Our interviewees reported that schools had a separate human resources system for accountability.
- Included the elements of K–12 public school teaching review systems that focused on instructional feedback: observations of teaching, reflection, conversations/feedback from observers about instructional practice and goals for continuous improvement, and student feedback.
- Used management software (Folio is a common one that was designed for use by independent schools) to make the review process transparent, create a record, and help manage all the observation notes and conversation notes in one place.
- Housed the teaching review process in academic departments. In all of the schools we spoke with, department chairs were the "keepers" of the teaching review process. Two independent school association staff said that they felt that, in the future, more schools would shift toward cross-departmental instructional coaches, but this is not a practice in use in the eight schools we interviewed. Instead, department chairs were responsible for such administrative tasks as scheduling (usually with the help of a dedicated administrator), observing teachers, performing instructional coaching, and holding feedback and goal-setting conversations.
- Employed an administrator whose job largely focused on ensuring the teaching review process occurred on schedule. This person was generally not a department chair or someone involved in doing observations.

Those we interviewed at independent schools or associations of independent schools shared the following lessons learned about revising teaching reviews and implementing the new systems. All of the principles of these lessons are supported by education research in K–12 public school settings.

- Keep the process and the tools simple. Complex teaching review processes can be difficult to communicate clearly, and that can result in faculty and administrators having different understandings of what the process entails. Complex processes can also be time-consuming and expensive to administer. In addition, a complex system can feel like a burdensome add-on, increasing the risk that the activities will get pushed aside. As one administrator said, "the daily grind of what you have to do always trumps teacher reviews." In addition, keep the review tools (e.g., observation form, student feedback form, self-reflection template) simple and aligned to the school's instructional vision and definition of good teaching.
- Focus on development and continuous improvement of teaching practice. All of the administrators with whom we spoke emphasized the importance of keeping the teaching review process developmental, safe, and low stakes. As one administrator said, "you must cultivate an environment in which teachers feel safe if you want them to be invested in growth." This guidance is consistent with recent K–12 research that has pointed out the challenges of focusing on development and professional growth in a system that also serves an accountability purpose (Kraft and Christian, 2021; Hunter and Springer, 2022; Stecher et al., 2018).
- Implement gradually. All the school administrators we interviewed said that they were building their cohesive instructional system from the ground up. Some had been engaged in the process for several years, while others were new to the work. But all planned for at least a five-year timeline. The school

administrators said that they piloted discrete tools or processes, adjusted, piloted again, and in general adopted new tools and processes gradually.
- Engage faculty early and often. All the administrators and experts we interviewed said that involving teachers in co-creating the teaching review process (as well as supporting elements, such as a definition of good teaching) was critical for success. The school administrators we spoke with described convening faculty committees, holding listening sessions, communicating frequently and through multiple channels, and cultivating faculty champions. Most schools described a department-driven development process complemented with school-wide, cross-department committees. School administrators organized the process, provided support, guidance, and a school-wide view. This approach meant that department chairs were often in the position of liaising between administrators and faculty, and several administrators urged that other schools recognize this work and create time for chairs to do it well.

To Be an Effective Developmental Tool, Classroom Observations Should Measure Specific, Observable Behaviors of Teachers, Be Simple Enough to Use, and Be Paired with High-Quality Feedback

All the postsecondary and K–12 public school literature we identified about teaching review systems—whether developmental or evaluative—included classroom observations as one element of review (Ross and Walsh, 2019; Schweig, 2019). So, too, did independent high schools whose leaders we interviewed. In some public school districts' evaluative systems, where teacher bonuses or retention decisions are based in part on observation ratings, it is critical that the observations be reliable and valid measures of teacher performance. These high stakes have prompted a large body of research on classroom observation tools and processes, some of which we summarize in this section.

The stakes in a developmental system like the one we recommend for Andover are lower. Nonetheless, it is still important that classroom observations provide actionable information to teachers in a manner that minimizes observer bias. So, while Andover need not meet the gold standard required in an evaluative system for observer training, number of observers, and number of observations,[3] we still recommend that Andover (1) remake its current classroom observation tool to include prompts that refer the observer to the desired student and teacher competencies, and (2) train all of the department chairs and associate chairs in its use.

In this section, we present lessons learned from the public school literature, which provides the most rigorous body of research on the subject about how to implement fair and reliable teacher observations for the dual purpose of enhancing professional learning and teacher accountability.

Classroom observations are well suited to provide quality feedback for teachers to help them improve their practice (Papay, 2012; Archer et al., 2016). In public schools, classroom observations typically serve developmental and evaluative purposes, as we have described. Using a standardized scoring instrument, an evaluator—such as a school administrator or instructional coach—rates teachers undergoing review against a set of key teaching dimensions or competencies. The resulting scores are used in aggregate with other measures of instruction, including student performance scores and data from student surveys, to quantify teaching performance and inform the professional learning of teachers through one-on-one feedback sessions between the observed and observer. Research shows that under specific conditions (i.e., using multiple observers over multiple observations), the composite scores on several popular scoring instruments (includ-

---

[3] The prevailing wisdom for use of classroom observation scores in evaluative systems is that teachers be observed by two different trained observers over a minimum of four observations annually (Putman et al., 2018; Prado Tuma, Hamilton, and Tsai, 2018; Ho and Kane, 2013; Kane and Staiger, 2012). Research also shows the importance of comprehensive training, certification, and regular recalibration exercises for evaluators (Archer et al., 2016; Ho and Kane, 2013; Cohen and Goldhaber, 2016).

ing the Danielson Framework for Teaching and CLASS) correlate with observed gains in student achievement, which provides some confidence that classroom observation tools measure classroom activities conducive to student learning (Kane and Staiger, 2012; Chaplin et al., 2014).

Danielson's Framework for Teaching and Marzano's Causal Teacher Evaluation are the most widely used scoring instruments in K–12 school systems (Close, Amrein-Beardsley, and Collins, 2020). As previously mentioned, to the degree that independent schools use commercial observation tools at all, interviewees told us the Danielson was the most common starting point, which most then went on to substantially shorten or only used as one of many examples. We include these in Table 3.1, where we summarize the most widely used commercially available observation tools and the constructs they measure.

In theory, each instrument rests on some understanding of what constitutes good instruction (Cohen and Goldhaber, 2016). Some instruments, including the Danielson Framework for Teaching, Marzano Causal Teacher Evaluation, and CLASS consist of non-content-specific elements of teaching. Other instruments (not reviewed here) emphasize content-specific instructional elements, which require raters to have specific knowledge of content (Cohen and Goldhaber, 2016). A comparison of five popular scoring instruments, including the Danielson Framework for Teaching and CLASS, found considerable overlap in their concepts. Namely, each of the instruments contained measures for at least eight out of the same ten dimensions of instructional practice: supportive learning environment, student focus, classroom management, student intellectual engagement with content, lesson structure, knowledge of content, language and discourse, and feedback and assessment (Gill et al., 2016).

The instruments also shared similar sources of bias in the ratings. For example, several studies have found that student characteristics impacted teachers' scores on both the Danielson and CLASS. Specifically, teachers assigned to classrooms with larger percentages of students in minoritized groups tended to receive reduced scores, but only in English language arts (Gill et al, 2016). Other studies demonstrate that teachers of students with higher performance levels from the previous year receive higher scores than teachers with lower performing students (Steinberg and Garrett, 2016). Multiple scholars have raised the possibility that some dimensions of practice on observation protocols may be more susceptible to bias than others based on student characteristics (Cohen and Goldhaber, 2016) and that failure to adjust for real differences in classroom composition, including student poverty, previous performance, and prior misconduct will lead to inherently biased ratings (Steinberg and Sartain, 2021).

Even with training and ongoing calibration, the scores of observers are still subject to "drift," which means that variability in ratings increases over time (Casabianca, Lockwood, and McCaffrey, 2015). Although the sources of rater bias are complex, research points to six common "observer effects" that may increase the likelihood of biased ratings (Archer et al., 2016; Joe et al., 2013):

1. prior familiarity between the observer and observed
2. the "halo" effect, which occurs when an observer inflates ratings based on the reputation of the teacher they are observing or strong performance in one category of practice
3. the "fatal flaw" effect, which is the opposite of the halo effect
4. the tendency of raters to give middle ratings (i.e., "central tendency" effect)
5. artificial inflation of scores when tied to perceived stakes
6. natural drift over time as raters increasingly impose their own personal interpretation of items over time.

Other research points to implicit sources of observer bias based on personal preferences, including biases based on a teacher's gender or race, the characteristics of the students they teach, or school characteristics (Campbell and Ronfeldt, 2018; Grissom and Bartanen, 2022; Steinberg and Sartain, 2021). In a study that used eight years of data from classroom observations collected in Tennessee, Grissom and Bartanen (2022)

TABLE 3.1
Characteristics of Commonly Used Observation Tools for High School Level

Name	What It Measures	Intended Frequency
Danielson's Framework for Teaching	• Planning and preparation • Classroom environment • Instruction • Professional Responsibilities	4 times yearly, at least 1 full
Danielson's Framework for Teaching Focus Series (Intellectual Engagement)	• Content knowledge and pedagogy • Knowing and valuing students • Planning coherent instruction • Fostering a culture for learning • Supporting positive behaviors • Communicating purpose and content • Questioning and discussion techniques • Engaging students in learning • Responding flexibly	Not specified
Teachstone's Classroom Assessment Scoring System (CLASS)	3 domains of teacher-student interactions: • Emotional support • Classroom organization • Instructional support	2 to 4 15-minute shorts over a 2-hour block
Marzano's Causal Teacher Evaluation Model (Rubric and Observation Tool)	• Standards-based planning • Standards-based instruction • Conditions for learning • Professional responsibilities	Not specified
National Institution for Excellence in Teaching (TAP Rubric)	• Planning • Instruction • Environment • Professionalism	3–4 times yearly
The New Teaching Project (TNTP Core)	• Culture of learning • Essential content • Academic ownership • Demonstration of learning	Not specified
McREL's Teacher Evaluation System (Content, Understanding, Environment, and Support Framework)	• Content • Understanding • Environment • Support	At least 3 times yearly for new teachers; at least once for veterans
The Marshall Rubric	• Planning and preparation • Classroom management • Delivery of instruction • Monitoring • Assessment • Follow-up • Family and community outreach • Professional responsibilities	
District of Columbia Public Schools Impact Model, The Five Essential Practices	• Cultivation of a responsive learning community • Challenging students with rigorous content • Leading a well-planned, purposeful learning experience • Maximizing student ownership of learning • Responding to evidence of student learning	1–3 times yearly, >30 minutes
Denver Public Schools' and Denver Classroom Teachers Association's Leading Effective Academic Practice Framework for Effective Teaching	• Learning Environment • Instruction • Professionalism	At least 2 observations yearly, 1 full-length plus up to 5 shorts

Table 3.1—continued

Name	What It Measures	Intended Frequency
Dallas Independent School District's Teacher Excellence Initiative, Teacher Performance Rubric	• Designing research-based, rigorous lessons for diverse populations • Developing and executing purposeful, highly effective, and rigorous instruction • Embracing a mindset of continuous improvement and accountability • Building safe, supportive, and rigorous learning environments	1 full-length and 4 shorts yearly

observed that, even after accounting for other measures of teachers' effectiveness, white and female teachers received higher scores than their Black and male counterparts. Campbell and Ronfeldt (2018) noted similar findings; however, they add that these differences may be driven by differences in how raters assign scores based on student characteristics. Specifically, teachers sorted into classrooms with more Black, Hispanic, male, low-income, and low-performing students tend to receive lower scores than their peers and teachers of color are more likely work in classrooms with low-income and lower achieving students (Kalogrides, Loeb, and Béteille, 2013; Campbell and Ronfeldt, 2018). In a study looking at the Black-White gap in ratings across public schools in Chicago, Steinberg and Sartain (2021) found that differences in scoring between teachers were due to school-level and contextual differences—including student poverty levels, previous academic performance, and previous student misconduct—not actual differences in teacher quality.

For developmental systems, the research indicates that the following standards are important for selection of a classroom observation tool. The instrument Andover ultimately uses—whether a commercially available, self-developed, or hybrid of the two—should reflect a shared understanding of good teaching and should measure *specific* observable behaviors of teachers in their classrooms (Gill et al., 2016; Joe et al., 2013). The research and our independent school interviews suggest that it is important to keep the tool simple to fill out; that is, it should only call for a record of just some faculty and student actions (Archer et al., 2016). Otherwise, observers may struggle to effectively juggle too many measures of teacher quality, especially those that are more content-specific (Cohen and Goldhaber, 2016).

Giving High-Quality Feedback to Teachers

Regardless of the observation tool, the value of classroom observations depends on the quality of feedback. High-quality feedback should focus on an area of growth, use concrete evidence as a basis for feedback, help teachers identify specific goals, and include actionable next steps (Hunter and Springer, 2022; Archer et al., 2016; Greenfield et al., 2022). Providing actionable feedback is not a given; one study of 1,200 public school teachers in Tennessee found that most of the feedback these teachers received as part of the classroom observations did not include these four components (Hunter and Springer, 2022).

In addition to following these guidelines, Archer et al. (2016) advises that schools should develop a shared vision for what effective feedback looks like, including

- guidance for pre- and post-observation conferences
- guidance for observers on how to help teachers integrate specific techniques into their instruction
- guidance on effective tone and how to modify feedback for different teachers
- training to practice providing feedback.

Detailed, constructive feedback should accompany every classroom observation (Putnam, Walsh, and Ross, 2018). In our review of large-scale K–12 evaluation systems, post-observation feedback was delivered either in writing or face-to-face. It is not uncommon for observers to provide written feedback to teachers following every observation, particularly after short observations (<15 minutes), and face-to-face feedback during a post-observation conference following only full-length (>45 minutes) observations. In addition to post-observation conferences, many school systems also require observers and teachers to engage in a pre-observation "goal setting" or "planning" meeting. Occasionally, teachers are asked to complete a written reflection as part of the process.

Post-observation conferences and written feedback should avoid starting off with direct criticism and overwhelming teachers with too many details (Archer et al., 2016). In selecting one area for growth, the literature suggests zeroing in on one technique or "bite-sized" target area for improvement (Archer et al., 2016; Hunter and Springer, 2022). In addition to training classroom observers, school administrators should develop protocols and provide training to teachers about how to give and receive constructive feedback (Timperley, 2015).

Classroom Observers Should Be Trained

Even in a low-stakes developmental system, it is still important to train observers about common sources of bias inherent in teacher observation systems and to refresh training for observers (e.g., department chairs) to avoid unfairly or mischaracterizing teachers' practices based on situational context or personal preferences. The six common sources of evaluator bias that we listed above (e.g., a preexisting relationship between the observer and the observed, "halo" and "fatal flaw" effects) plus biases related to classroom context or the teacher's own characteristics can consciously and unconsciously influence observation ratings, notes, and feedback.

The first step in mitigating these and other sources of bias is to establish a clear definition of *bias* and refer to the definition often, either in trainings or staff meetings and on the observation tool itself. Observers should be trained and encouraged to reflect on sources of personal bias in addition to the sources of bias mentioned above (Archer et al., 2016).

The literature we reviewed recommends using pre-scored videos to establish and illustrate proficiency across teaching competencies. As a form of norming, before observing teachers and providing feedback, new observers should demonstrate the ability to match their scores against pre-scored videos or those provided by an expert observer (Archer et al., 2016; Ho and Kane, 2013).

Student Surveys Offer Useful Formative Feedback, But the Risk of Biases in Them Should Limit Which Kinds of Questions to Ask for High-Stakes Use

Here we reviewed K–12 and postsecondary literature and looked to literature from healthcare about patient satisfaction surveys and management to inform our recommendations to Andover for student surveys. Our intent in this section was to identify how Andover can collect student feedback on surveys in a way that maximizes their value for teachers for instructional decisionmaking while minimizing the sources of bias documented in the postsecondary literature.

Decades of research has demonstrated both the benefits and limitations of relying on student feedback as a measure of how well teachers are targeting instruction towards their intended audience and impacting student learning. Currently, 27 percent of states use or encourage the use of student surveys in K–12 systems as one of multiple measures of teaching performance (Close, Amrein-Beardsley, and Collins, 2020). Use of student feedback surveys is also widespread in postsecondary institutions (Richardson, 2005) and increasingly common in independent schools. In 2011, for example, the National Association of Independent Schools partnered with Indiana University's Center for Evaluation and Education Policy to study the use of the High School Survey of Student Engagement (HSSSE) in independent schools, which it now offers to all its member schools (Torres, 2016). The HSSSE collects school-wide (rather than class-specific) information about students' attitude, perceptions, beliefs, and school experiences.

Our take based on the literature is that student surveys—whether centrally adopted or developed by teachers—are extremely helpful for low-stakes, developmental use, such as teachers' continuous improvement of their instructional practice.

In contrast, the consensus in the K–12 and postsecondary literature is that student surveys should not be used without corroboration for evaluative or high-stakes judgments about a teachers' performance (Rollett, Bijlsma, and Röhl, 2021; Gravestock and Gregor-Greenleaf, 2008). Teachers express concerns about using student feedback for high-stakes purposes (Linse, 2017); for instance, students are not in the best position to comment on some aspects of teaching, and student responses may unintentionally reflect their implicit biases about instructors (Peterson et al., 2019).

Student Surveys for Developmental Uses

The K–12 research and postsecondary research agree that student feedback is an important source of formative information about teaching (Kane and Cantrell, 2010; Schweig and Martínez, 2021; Göllner, Fauth and Wagner, 2021; Linse, 2017; Theall and Franklin, 2000; Richardson, 2005). In addition to giving students a voice—which has its own benefits (Wisniewski and Zierer, 2021)—student feedback, when gathered for low-stakes, developmental uses, can give teachers timely, actionable data that they can use to improve their teaching (Theall and Franklin, 2000). For example, student feedback surveys can help teachers understand how different groups of students (e.g., students of color, students with disabilities) experience their instruction and the overall learning environment, assuming that an anonymous student survey also collects information about the students' race or ethnicity (Schweig and Martinez, 2021). The results can also help a teacher identify improvements in practice, such as learning that students perceive the teacher as talking more than they are aware or providing explanations that students find confusing (Wisniewski and Zierer, 2021).

Student surveys are cost- and time-efficient (Geiger and Amrein-Beardsley, 2019) and allow teachers insight into aspects of their instruction not readily observed by adults (Wisniewski and Zierer, 2021). Some postsecondary scholars argue that students are in the best position to report on some teacher behaviors, such as the teacher's availability and responsiveness to questions, the amount of work required in a course, whether the teacher adequately explains the material, and timeliness and helpfulness of feedback (Theall and Franklin, 2001; Linse, 2017; McKeachie, 1990; Gravestock and Gregor-Greenleaf, 2008). Students can also provide time-sensitive feedback to teachers about assignments and units of study under development to allow a teacher to adapt their instruction accordingly.

However, the postsecondary literature acknowledges that students are not the best sources of information about all topics related to teaching. They do not, for example, have the expertise to evaluate the instructor's knowledge of the curriculum, appropriate pedagogical practices, or fairness of grading practices (Uttl, White, and Gonzalez, 2017; Geiger and Amrein-Beardsley, 2019; Gravestock and Gregor-Greenleaf, 2008; Theall and Franklin, 2001).

Student Surveys for Higher-Stakes Uses

Anonymous student surveys to ensure that courses meet basic professional standards should be implemented carefully in light of the concerns about using student feedback for high-stakes purposes. Even when narrowed to solely factual questions about the course, a student survey should not be the only source of information about whether a teacher or course meets professional standards (Theall and Franklin, 2000, 2001). Instead, we propose that a school-wide anonymous student survey about courses serve as a way to surface issues for teachers and department chairs to address and, if not resolved, to potentially lead to subsequent investigation using other data sources.

Even for this limited purpose, the questions on this survey would need to be constructed carefully so that they focused on yielding actionable information about the aspects of teaching and the course that students are in the best position to comment on, as we discuss below. Given teacher concerns about the use of student surveys for high-stakes purposes, we recommend that Andover seek teacher input on item selection and development.

We believe that the postsecondary research about student feedback on surveys about courses are the most relevant to Andover because the surveys are similar in content and used for similar purposes. This body of research documents several sources of bias in student responses (Peterson et al., 2019), and it also points to some ways to reduce but not entirely eliminate bias. For example, there is evidence that implicit student biases based on teacher race, ethnicity, or gender can result in lower ratings for female teachers or teachers of color (Storage et al., 2016; Boring, Ottoboni, and Stark, 2016; Mengel, Sauermann, and Zölitz, 2019; Fan et al., 2019; MacNell, Driscoll, and Hunt, 2015; Peterson et al., 2019). In addition, there is some evidence that students' course ratings can be influenced by factors such as students' prior interests, class size and content area, whether the course is required or not, whether the course is in STEM (science, technology, engineering, and mathematics) or humanities, a teacher's perceived attractiveness, whether the instructor is U.S.-born, course difficulty, and grade expectations (Hornstein, 2017; Kreitzer and Sweet-Cushman, 2021; Uttl, 2021).

There are also other sources of measurement error in student survey feedback including non-random sorting of students into different classrooms, lower response rates for some types of students, and halo-rating or general impression errors such as students marking a teacher high or low on all items (Geiger and Amrein-Beardsley, 2019). However, these concerns about measurement bias are most salient when student feedback surveys are used in high-stakes teacher evaluation settings.

The good news is that there are strategies to minimize these sources of bias. The first step in minimizing bias and improving the usability of student survey data is to embed student feedback structures into what is already a healthy culture of teaching and learning that values feedback (Röhl and Gärtner, 2021). Part of this work includes preparing students to engage in the exchange of productive feedback. For example, Fleenor (2021) points to two common pitfalls in employee feedback that schools should work to avoid: unclear purpose and lack of organizational readiness. Specifically, raters (in this case, students) are more likely to provide honest information if they believe their feedback *matters* to those in authority, if they perceive the process as useful, and if they do not fear retaliation (Smith and Fortunato, 2008; Richardson, 2005). Put another way, the purpose of the feedback should be transparent and there should be evidence that teachers or the school act in response to it (Wisniewski and Zierer, 2021).

An extensive body of health care survey research to replace subjective patient satisfaction surveys with more objective and reliable ratings of care suggests several lessons that apply to student surveys (Agency for Healthcare Research and Quality, undated):

- Write standardized, specific, close-ended items about specific activities for which students are the best source of information, such as the time it takes them to complete homework during a specified reference period such as the past week. Avoid asking questions about information that teachers or the school could gather from elsewhere.
- If using open-ended items, use them as a way to understand scores from close-ended items more fully or to pinpoint areas for improvement rather than as a replacement for close-ended items.
- To maximize the usefulness of the results, ask about only those questions that the teacher or school feels is important to the conduct of the class.
- Avoid summative questions about teachers (e.g., "Is this a good teacher?") and instead ask questions that will yield actionable information for teachers or the school.

The postsecondary literature echoes these lessons. In their comprehensive review, Gravestock and Gregor-Greenleaf (2008) caution against asking students to provide feedback on subjective aspects of teaching (e.g., enthusiasm or approachability of the teacher), recommend that questions ask about topics that students are knowledgeable about and for which there are no other sources of information (e.g., the amount of time students spend on course assignments each week), and advise that the questions be closely aligned to the institution's definition of good teaching, and address aspects of teaching that are within the control of the teacher to change if desired.

When used for high-stakes purposes, schools should also enact strict protocols for how student feedback surveys are distributed, proctored, and collected (Kane and Staiger, 2012). The postsecondary literature suggests that asking teachers to read a script before administering the feedback survey can mitigate bias based on teacher race and ethnicity or gender in student feedback on STEM and non-STEM courses (Peterson et al., 2019; see Box 3.1 for an example).

Instructors can also provide training to students on how to provide feedback (Göbel et al., 2021). While this is an ongoing area of research, the literature suggests that part of the reason students may struggle to provide constructive feedback is that they have not had enough practice doing so (Svinicki, 2001). The limited research we found suggests that because feedback is a skill, it is best learned by observing a good model (Svinicki, 2001; Bandura, 1986). For example, teachers might model examples of constructive and unconstructive criticism in response to a hypothetical survey question to prime students prior to administering a survey.

Teachers' concerns about using student surveys for purposes other than developmental feedback vary. Linse (2017) provides a comprehensive list of common concerns, which includes worries that some faculty manipulate students to achieve higher ratings; that students do not take the ratings seriously, lie, or are overly critical; that students do not understand effective teaching methods; and that, when using the data, administrators focus only on negative ratings without considering the full variation in responses (see also Gravestock and Gregor-Greenleaf, 2008).

Some of these concerns can be mitigated by the strategies to minimize student bias we discuss above (e.g., training students, use of scripts, careful selection of question topics). Linse (2017) offers detailed strategies for

---

BOX 3.1

Example Text for a Pre-Survey Script

Your anonymous feedback about this class helps Andover administrators know whether the course is operating as intended so the school can quickly address any issues that may arise. This survey asks a limited range of questions about the class; your teacher will separately solicit your feedback about other important aspects of this course.

Student evaluations of teaching are often influenced by students' unconscious and unintentional biases about the race and gender of the instructor. Historically, women and instructors of color are systematically rated lower in their teaching evaluations than white men, even when there are no actual differences in the instruction.

As you fill out the course evaluation please keep this in mind and make an effort to resist stereotypes about faculty. Focus on the content of the course (the assignments, the textbook, the in-class material) and not unrelated matters (the instructor's appearance or demeanor).

SOURCE: Adapted from Peterson et al., 2019.

responding to teacher concerns, which include clearly defining how the student feedback is used and involving teachers in survey design to increase trust and buy-in.

Other Considerations for Survey Design

Whether for low- or high-stakes uses, surveys should be kept to a reasonable length to avoid survey fatigue, which may lead to less-thoughtful responses (English et al., 2015; Meade and Craig, 2012). Most commercially available surveys we identified take students 10–15 minutes complete.

Survey wording is also important. Students should be able to easily discern what is being asked. Items should ask about one thing as opposed to several, which creates confusion for students about which part of the question to rate when providing their answer and for teachers in how to interpret the results and items should avoid double negatives (Kane and Staiger, 2012).

Quality Professional Learning That Adheres to Best Practices Can Support System Coherence and Continuous Improvement of Teaching Practice

Although a large body of research addresses the principles of effective professional learning for teachers in K–12 public schools, there is little research that speaks to professional learning in independent schools or in postsecondary institutions (Cormas et al., 2021). Therefore, we focus on summarizing the K–12 public school research in this section.

Professional learning activities that are aligned to the curriculum and to the school's common instructional vision are a key component of a coherent instructional system and should promote continuous instructional improvement. Our conceptualization of professional learning includes feedback after observations and peer reviews of teaching.

Research on K–12 public school teachers' professional learning suggests that effective, high-quality professional learning opportunities share a common set of features. In general, they focus on the content of the subject or academic discipline; are aligned to classroom activities; provide opportunities for active learning, practice, and ongoing feedback; involve participation of a group of teachers from the same school, department, or grade; are supported by administrators; and are sustained over time (Archibald et al., 2011; Coggshall et al., 2012; Garet et al., 2001; Yoon et al., 2007; Desimone, 2009; Popova et al., 2022).

Another aspect of effective professional learning is teachers' respect for the source of the learning and trust in its purpose. Teachers who do not believe that the provider of the professional learning activity or the source of the feedback (e.g., an instructional coach) is qualified to understand and accurately observe both the subject matter and pedagogy at hand, and that the activity serves only a developmental purpose, are likely to resist making changes to their instruction (Stecher et al., 2018). Not surprisingly, teachers are less likely to respond favorably to feedback if they do not perceive it to be accurate or useful (Cherasaro et al., 2016; Feeney, 2007; Garubo and Rothstein, 1998). And teachers tend to find feedback that is focused on instructional skills to be the most helpful (Prado Tuma, Hamilton, and Tsai, 2018).

Instructional coaching has become an increasingly popular type of professional development in K–12 public schools. K–12 schools might offer coaching to all teachers and/or might provide coaching to teachers who have developed specific goals for professional growth as part of their teaching evaluation. Our interviews and literature review suggest that it is not yet as common in independent schools. We summarize the literature about instructional coaching because it has been shown to be effective. But we note that the majority of Andover faculty who participated in ExpertLens process that we explain in chapter 4 expressed strong skepticism about cross-departmental and even within-division instructional coaches (instead endorsing department chairs over the idea of using an Andover teacher trained as an instructional coach).

Although there are various models for providing instructional coaching, the K–12 literature describes effective coaching as an ongoing collaborative partnership between teachers and pedagogical experts that is "individualized, time-intensive, sustained over the course of a semester or year, context-specific, and focused on discrete skills" (Blazar, 2020). Not only is instructional coaching of this type one of the fastest growing forms of job-embedded professional development, but it is also effective (Blazar, 2020; Gibbons and Cobb, 2017). According to a recent meta-analysis, the positive impacts of coaching on a K–12 public school teacher's practice amounts to more than the difference in instructional quality between novice teachers compared with their veteran peers (Kraft, Blazar and Hogan, 2018). Here we summarize what is known about the most promising practices for instructional coaching.

Institutional conditions and roles: Although instructional coaching has increased in popularity, it is not universally accepted by teachers (Woulfin, 2020). A 2020 study of coaching programs in three separate school systems found that teachers' acceptance of coaching largely depended on how adeptly school leaders "strategically framed" the purpose of coaching and enmeshed coaching structures into the fabric of existing routines and policies (Woulfin, 2020). In other words, teachers must view coaching as normal and not as a remedial action for just some teachers. Beyond this, coaches should have a strong command of their content area and sufficient classroom experience of at least five to eight years (Gibbons and Cobb, 2017; White et al., 2015). Coaches are typically accomplished teachers in a specific discipline (Poglinco et al., 2003). Teachers should possess a working knowledge of their subject, be willing participants, and demonstrate commitment to improved student outcomes (White et al., 2015).

What makes coaching effective: Instructional coaching should (1) emphasize content, (2) actively involve teachers in their own learning, (3) be aligned with instructional goals, including student and teacher competencies, (4) be ongoing and sustained, and (5) involve collective participation among teachers (Garet et al., 2001). In their review of coaching practices that meet these objectives, Gibbons and Cobb (2017) identify six specific coaching practices as especially promising: (1) deeply engaging teachers as learners of their own content, (2) shared examination of student work, (3) independent and mutual reflection based on video-based classroom observations, (4) participation in lesson study, (5) co-teaching, and (6) modeling.

Coaching is an iterative process: Instructional coaching is fundamentally relational, requiring intentional cultivation of mutual respect and trust over time. Exchanges should be content-centered and based on positive feedback (White et al., 2015). In the context of mutually trusting relationships, teachers and coaches can work toward a common set of goals. While coaches may engage teachers in a variety of activities, the essence of their role is one-on-one instructional support based on iterative cycles of observation and feedback. White et al. (2015) suggest a simple model for successful progression through what they call the Goal-Directed Coaching Process. First, the teacher and coach should jointly agree on a set of goals, including next steps before the next meeting or observation (planning phase). Next, the teacher and coach engage in an action or practice stage, which involves opportunities, including those suggested by Gibbons and Cobb (2017), to develop targeted skills. Third, coaches and teachers should review video-based classroom observations of teachers. Fourth, teachers should engage in self-reflection followed by feedback and reflective discussion.

Making a Coherent Instructional System Work in Practice

In this section, we summarize lessons learned about implementing a large-scale change such as building a coherent instructional system in a school. We discuss best practices and strategies to avoid based on the K–12 public school literature about teaching reviews, the literature on public-sector performance management systems, and our interviews of staff at independent schools.

The high-level lessons from these sources of information are to design a system that teachers will realistically buy into, to allot five or even more years to get all the elements in place, to hire a project manager and reallocate assignments and responsibilities as needed to provide staff sufficient time to design and execute

Teacher Buy-In Is Essential to Successful Change

New school initiatives—particularly those that involve reviews of or adjustments to teaching—may be doomed to fail if teachers are not involved in their development and implementation (Stecher et al., 2018; Cook et al., 2019; Yoon, 2016; Zimmerman, 2006; Desimone, 2002). For example, in a major eight-year study of teaching evaluation reforms in nine K–12 public school systems, limited teacher buy-in was a key reason for failed implementation (Stecher et al., 2018). Likewise, the independent school administrators and experts we interviewed, and the postsecondary literature, confirmed the critical importance of teacher buy-in when developing and implementing new teacher and student competencies, teaching review processes and tools, and departmental review activities (Kang et al., 2022; Furco and Moely, 2012).

Education leaders can promote teacher buy-in through the following strategies:

- Take a collaborative approach, in which employees are involved in the design of new systems and processes (Greenfield et al., 2022; Stecher et al., 2010).
- Adopt an iterative approach to developing and refining systems and processes in which ideas are generated using both bottom-up and top-down approaches, tested in pilot projects, and adopted in phases (Greenfield et al., 2022; Stecher et al., 2010).
- Clearly communicate through multiple channels, which could involve face-to-face meetings, drop-in office hours, email, newsletters, and trainings (Greenfield et al. 2022, Stecher, et al., 2010).

Give Faculty and Departments Time to Meet

Of course, departments need the time to meet to develop—and eventually to update—student competencies, teaching review tools, and student feedback surveys, and to engage in departmental review activities. Most of the independent schools we interviewed emphasized the importance of faculty collaboration within departments and on cross-department committees to develop components of the coherent instructional system, and they said it was necessary for administrators to provide enough time in the schedule for meaningful collaboration.

Mercersburg Academy, for example, leveraged its COVID-19-era infrastructure for asynchronous learning to encourage departments to schedule one asynchronous learning day per quarter. On this day, the departments cancelled in-person classes and students were instead asked to work independently outside the classroom on asynchronous assignments, while faculty took the half day for planning, course development, and other department activities. In another example, Pomfret School paid its faculty to engage in a week of professional learning time in the summer, during which departments were expected to plan, design, and align their courses for the next year.

Developing and implementing a coherent instructional system is a multi-year process in both the research about implementation in public schools (Stecher et al., 2018) and in the independent schools whose leaders we interviewed. All the independent school experts and administrators we interviewed said that creating a process for departmental review is a multiyear process, especially when combined with the other activities that schools are pursuing to develop a coherent instructional system, such as revamping their process for peer review of teaching, developing teacher and student competencies, and aligning professional development. Our interviewees also acknowledged that the process of creating a coherent instructional system was, in the words of one administrator we interviewed, "really messy, and not linear." Our interviewees advised administrators in other schools to recognize that this work is time-consuming, to be prepared for some faculty members to perceive it as an additional obligation in an already busy schedule, and to intentionally create enough time for the work.

Likewise, in the K–12 and postsecondary literature we reviewed, time constraints and expectation of excessive time commitments were the top organizational barriers to faculty buy-in and implementation of organizational change and professional learning activities (Desimone, 2002; Furco and Moely, 2012; Gast, Schildkamp, and van der Veen, 2017). Especially in the early stages of inquiry-driven processes, failure to allow sufficient time for faculty to explore root causes may result in the premature selection of an intervention before defining the problem they are trying to solve (Copland, 2003). Moreover, creating common planning time for faculty to meet and collaborate during the day is associated with stronger professional ties and faculty buy-in to school-wide improvement initiatives (Desimone, 2002).

Institutional Commitment Is Also Key

The approach school leaders take to curriculum and school reform initiatives significantly influences teacher buy-in and implementation (Desimone, 2002; Yoon, 2016). School administrators can increase the likelihood that faculty will cooperate and collaborate successfully by focusing on five key "ingredients": vision, leadership, institutional commitment, resources, and incentives (Bohen and Stiles, 1998). Specifically:

- **Vision:** A school needs to develop a shared understanding for why change is needed and what problem will these changes address. The vision should be structured so as to inspire faculty participation by encouraging them to think about what is possible.
- **Leadership:** It is important to identify strong faculty leaders who, through whatever characteristics—their experience, reputation, commitment—can inspire other faculty to participate. These are known as "teacher leaders" in the K–12 literature, and researchers describe the importance of redefining their responsibilities and decisionmaking powers as a precondition for the type of democratic collaboration that leads to school improvement (Datnow and Castellano, 2001).
- **Institutional commitment:** School leaders should develop and maintain new structures to support faculty leaders, including effective governance and accountability protocols to guide the initiative. School leaders should consider offering faculty release time, incentives, and removing administrative hurdles.
- **Financial resources:** School leaders should consider in advance possible costs associated with the initiative (e.g., bringing on additional staff like a project manager, faculty compensation for increased workload, updated technology, etc.) and plan accordingly.
- **Incentives and rewards:** Collaborative reform takes time, and it is unreasonable to expect faculty to work overtime without allocated, compensated time to do it. While faculty may be willing to contribute initially, in the long term, additional uncompensated expectations may erode their commitment.

Complexity Lowers the Likelihood of Implementation

The K–12 public school literature and independent school leaders whom we interviewed agree that keeping the teaching review process simple is crucial to its long-term success. A simple process entails tools that are relatively quick to train staff to use, easy to use in practice, and require a reasonable and therefore sustainable time commitment—ideally no more than 2–3 hours per reviewer for each faculty member they formally review instead of the 5–12 hours per person that Andover department chairs estimated the formal reviews required.

Several independent school administrators said they initially planned to use commercially available observation tools, such as the Danielson Framework for Teaching, but upon reflection and discussion with faculty decided to develop their own tools because common commercial tools were too complex and time-consuming to administer. Similarly, over time many K–12 public school systems have reduced the number of observations and simplified their observation tools to reduce burden (Stecher et al., 2018).

Complex review processes based on long rubrics can cause unnecessary stress for those being observed. Moreover, the management literature points to an inverse relationship between complexity and desired results (Elmore, 1979). Elmore (1979) notes that with complexity comes an increased likelihood of "diversion and delay," combined with a decrease in independent problem solving.

When classroom observation rubrics are used as a tool for accountability, some experts recommend restructuring complicated rubrics into simpler "checks" to ensure that teachers are fulfilling basic obligations (Dynarski, 2016; Berliner, 2018). When classroom observation rubrics are used for developmental purposes, as explained by Ferlazzo (2022), "A great observation results in a conversation that creates a positive change in teacher performance. It is that simple." The goal for teacher observations, as we have described, is for teachers to walk out of their post-observation meetings with a single insight or a simple strategy they can put directly to use (Archer et al., 2016).

CHAPTER 4

Andover Faculty Views About Potential Policy Revisions

This chapter summarizes faculty reactions during spring 2022 to the potential recommendations we posed about ways to revise Andover's teaching review policies and departmental self-reviews.

To gather faculty feedback about potential changes, we conducted a three-round online modified Delphi process. Delphi is a RAND-developed approach to consensus-building that is based on iterative and anonymous data collection and sharing of intermediate findings with participants (Dalkey and Helmer, 1963). In round 1, faculty rated 14 potential policy changes (written by the research team) and provided brief explanations about their ratings. Then several weeks later, in round 2, faculty viewed their collective ratings and comments from round 1. Round 2 was a discussion round in which faculty responded asynchronously and anonymously to questions we posed in a discussion board format. Faculty could also pose questions and comments to each other. In round 3, faculty re-rated five revised recommendations that we wrote based on faculty feedback from rounds 1 and 2. To conduct the online Delphi process, we used a RAND-created online platform called ExpertLens (Dalal et al., 2011). We provide more details about the Delphi process, ExpertLens and the methods for analysis of the faculty responses in Appendix A.

Key Takeaways

- While 72 percent of Andover faculty participated in at least one of three rounds of faculty feedback about potential recommendations we posed, participation dropped to only 39 percent by round 3, limiting the generalizability of the faculty ratings to our revised recommendations.
- In round 1, teachers endorsed four of the 14 proposals we posed, and they were uncertain or disagreed about the rest. Of the 14 potential recommendations, teachers endorsed the department- and faculty-led ideas, and they disapproved of proposals to centralize policy such as by creating an instructional coach role to lead the teaching review process rather than department chairs.
- By the end of the third round, Andover teachers rated four out of the five revised recommendations as helpful. Teachers of color rated the recommendations most positively, endorsing all five recommendations as helpful. White teachers endorsed two of the five and they were split (with high and low ratings) about the student competencies recommendation and were uncertain about identifying desired teacher competencies and revising the school-wide student survey.
- In general, teachers expressed skepticism about top-down or school-wide policy development, and instead placed greater trust in their departments.

Participation Rates

We invited all 158 teaching faculty at Andover who are subject to the teaching review policy described in Chapter 2 to participate in the ExpertLens process. Of those, 113 (72 percent) participated in at least one Delphi round. As is typical for Delphi panels, participation was highest in the first round and declined over the next two rounds, as shown in Table 4.1. Participation dropped to only 39 percent by round 3,[1] which was lower than we had hoped, limiting the generalizability of the final ratings from round 3.

In round 1, we did not see any large differences in the demographic characteristics of those faculty who participated and faculty who did not, as shown in Table 4.2. However, by round 3, when fewer faculty participated, some moderate-sized differences emerge. The largest difference was an over-representation of veteran

TABLE 4.1
Faculty Participation in Three Rounds of ExpertLens

Round	Date	Proportion of Faculty Who Participated
Round 1: Rate potential recommendations	February 14–March 4, 2022	63% (100 out of 158 invited)
Round 2: Review and discuss round 1 results	March 28–April 8, 2022	48% (76 out of 158) reviewed; 45% (34 out of 76) posted
Round 3: Rate revised potential recommendations	April 21–May 5, 2022	39% (61 out of 158)
Total of rounds 1–3	February 14–May 5, 3022	72% (113 out of 158 who participated in at least 1 round)

NOTE: Participation in rounds 1 and 3 is defined as providing one or more ratings.

TABLE 4.2
Participation Rates by Faculty Demographic Categories

Category	Overall Teaching Faculty (n = 158)		Faculty Who Participated in Round 1 (n = 100)		Faculty Who Participated in Round 3 (n = 61)	
	Number	%	Number	%	Number	%
Teachers of color	49	31	28	28	15	25
White	109	69	72	72	46	75
Less than 10 years of teaching at Andover	68	43	47	47	19	31
10 or more years	90	57	53	53	42	69
Female	79	50	54	54	31	51
Male	79	50	46	46	30	49

NOTE: Participation in rounds 1 and 3 is defined as providing one or more ratings.

---

[1] We hypothesize that there were three potential reasons participation dropped to 39 percent. (1) Round 1 took too much time to complete, and faculty were discouraged from further participation. (2) We fielded our questions in spring 2022, which was the third school year during the COVID-19 pandemic. Nationally representative surveys show that teacher morale substantially declined over the course of the pandemic (Steiner et al., 2022), and Andover administrators told us that Andover teachers also felt exhausted and had low morale. (3) We received comments from two individuals that some faculty were intentionally not participating to signal their disagreement with the content of the proposed recommendations that we asked faculty to rate. We do not know how common this practice was.

faculty, defined as those teachers with ten or more years of experience at Andover (69 percent of round 3 participants versus 57 percent of the overall teaching faculty). That meant that faculty with less than a decade of experience at Andover were under-represented. White faculty were also somewhat over-represented in round 3 (75 percent of round 3 participants versus 69 percent of faculty overall) and faculty of color were under-represented (25 percent of round 3 participants versus 31 percent overall).

Results from Rounds 1 and 2

In the first round, we posed 14 potential recommendations for the faculty to rate and comment upon. We proposed that Andover identify desired student and teacher competencies and that the Evaluation Committee shift to become an instructional coach committee, which would lead the faculty teaching review process. (Department chairs now handle those reviews.)

We developed these 14 potential recommendations based on the literature review contained in Chapter 3, the themes we learned from the Andover department chairs outlined in Chapter 2, and the interviews we conducted of independent schools described in Chapter 3. The full wording of each potential recommendation and ratings are in Table A.2 in Appendix A.

We asked faculty to rate each recommendation on two scales: "How helpful would this recommendation be for your development as a teacher?" and "How feasible do you think this recommendation would be for Andover to execute?" A score of 1 corresponded to "not at all helpful" or "not at all feasible" and a score of 9 corresponded to "very helpful" or "very feasible." After each numeric rating, faculty were asked to provide a brief comment explaining their response.

For brevity, the topics for each recommendation and faculty's median rating of the question "How helpful would this recommendation be for your development as a teacher?" are listed in Table 4.3. We truncated in the table the potential recommendation topic; the Appendix Table A.2 shows the full wording, which provided more context. In Table 4.3, we present the helpfulness ratings only because the feasibility ratings were highly correlated, and because we later dropped the feasibility question from round 3 to reduce the time required of faculty.

As shown in Table 4.3, faculty endorsed four of the 14 recommendations as helpful for their teaching, and they were uncertain or disagreed about the rest. Faculty had clear and positive consensus about:

- faculty fielding their own student surveys (potential recommendation 11)
- faculty observing at least one class of a fellow teacher in their department each year (potential recommendation 13)
- departments selecting a self-study topic each year (potential recommendation 12)
- faculty writing their self-reflection at the end rather than the beginning of the periodic teaching review cycle (potential recommendation 9).

Faculty had widely diverging views about the rest of the recommendations, resulting in a rating of "uncertain" helpfulness because their median ratings fell between 3.5 and 6 on the 1–9 scale or "disagreement" because more than a third of participants rated a recommendation as either not helpful (median ratings of 1–3.5) and helpful (median ratings of 6.5–9) at the same time.

TABLE 4.3
Faculty Ratings in Round 1 About the Helpfulness of a Policy Change for Their Teaching

Potential Recommendation Topic	Median Helpfulness Rating	Faculty Overall Determination
1: Create student competencies	5.5	Uncertain
2: Train elected teaching faculty to be instructional coaches who would lead the teacher development process	5	Uncertain
3: Meet with instructional coach each year to discuss their goals for that year	5	Uncertain
4: Every few years, receive a more comprehensive teaching review	6	Uncertain
5: Hold the comprehensive teaching review every three years	5	Uncertain
6: Create teacher competencies	6	Uncertain
7: Integrate student and teacher competencies into the teaching review process	5	Disagreement
8: Have instructional coaches lead the periodic teaching review	4	Uncertain
9: Write the self-reflection at the end of the teaching review rather than the beginning	7	Helpful
10: Repurpose the school-wide anonymous student survey to focus on minimum course expectations	5	Uncertain
11: Have faculty field their own student surveys each year, separate from and in addition to the anonymous school-wide student survey	9	Helpful
12: Select a self-study topic each year in each department	7	Helpful
13: Observe at least one class of another faculty member within their department each year	9	Helpful
14: Invite external observers to support departments' self-study process	6	Uncertain

NOTE: All 158 faculty were invited to rate each recommendation on a range of 1 to 9, where 1 was "not at all helpful" and 9 was "very helpful." The full wording of each potential recommendation is shown in Table A.2. As described in Appendix A, the faculty overall determination is calculated automatically by an ExpertLens algorithm based on the distribution of teacher ratings, and there are four potential determinations: helpful; uncertain helpfulness; unhelpful; disagreement.

Despite the divergence in faculty ratings about most of the recommendations, a few clear themes still emerged from the discussion comments faculty posted in ExpertLens:

- Most faculty did not like the instructional coach concept; instead, most faculty wanted to be evaluated by peers from their discipline and mistrusted the ability of those outside their discipline to adequately or fairly evaluate them.
- Most faculty placed significantly greater trust in bottom-up department-centric initiatives than in top-down school-wide processes. They also felt department-generated policy about teaching or evaluation would be more feasible to implement than a school-wide policy.
- Most faculty reacted negatively to recommendations that they perceived as limiting their autonomy.
- Many faculty comments indicate that they felt they were overworked; any policy that requires significant new time should be made up for by a reduction in some other part of their workload.
- Many faculty were skeptical that they could collectively agree on such school-wide initiatives like identifying desired student or teacher competencies.
- Faculty were skeptical that school-wide initiatives would actually be implemented.
- Faculty were skeptical that school-wide initiatives would be useful in practice.

Faculty also let us know that it took far longer than the 30 minutes we had requested to complete round 1. Therefore, to shorten our requests of faculty time in round 2, we posed six open-ended questions about only the most negatively rated recommendations to facilitate a focused exchange of ideas on these potential recommendations. However, faculty were free to pose their own comments and questions in the discussion round, and many did. In Table 4.4, we list the questions we posed during round 2 in the left-hand column and summarize with bullets in the right-hand column the main themes in faculty reactions with some indented supporting details. We include in Table 4.4 only the ideas that at least two or more faculty raised during the discussion.

TABLE 4.4
Faculty Reactions to Six Questions About Ways to Modify the Most Controversial Proposed Changes from Round 1

Discussion Question	Themes in Faculty Comments
Developing core student and teacher competencies at the department level first instead of at the school level	

Regarding recommendation 1 about developing student competencies: Would you support a revised recommendation that each department develop, update, or re-approve department-specific student competencies that would be in addition to a school-wide set of student competencies. The school-wide competencies would be derived in part from the department-specific competencies to create the portrait of an Andover graduate that NEASC recommended.	• So long as the identification of competencies starts with departments instead of school-level, this can be good. But . . .
	  – avoid a list of school-wide competencies that are "overly prescriptive"
	  – the process for developing this list needs to be democratic and involve full faculty participation with a clear and fair process
	  – "It would be fabulous to have department/division days dedicated to the development of discipline-specific content and skill competencies."
	• Department-specific student competencies are good and needed, but school-wide ones are not needed, as they would be:
	  – "too vague to be meaningful" or "performative"
	  – unnecessary; graduation requirements should suffice
	  – limiting of teachers' ability to nurture the diversity of needs and interests of each student
	• Inclusion of social and emotional competency standards is "problematic at best, and potentially very harmful. How would we assess them and what would we do if a student is found not to have met them?"

Regarding recommendation 6 about developing desired teacher competencies: Do you support a two-pronged approach to developing teacher competencies: (1) departments would develop department-specific teacher competencies, and (2) a school committee would develop a short list of core school-wide desired teacher competencies? Both would be a point of reference in the periodic teaching reviews. If not, are there alternatives you would support?	• Faculty expressed mostly similar concerns and responses as to the development of student competencies. The exception is that a few faculty supported the idea of starting first at the school level:
	  – "I feel like doing this via department is too hard. Instead, a central committee or task force could work on designing these competencies. Departments could take the competencies and customize them."
	  – "I would centralize this initially (committee plus full faculty discussion), write the competencies in plain language, and devote PD [professional development] time in departments to understanding and articulating how to implement them."
	• So long as the identification of competencies starts with departments instead of school-level, this can be good. But...
	  – "I worry that we will create a set of competencies that are unquantifiable and lose sight of the importance of RELATING to kids."
	  – "Fine, as long as the school-wide competencies emerge from broad faculty discussion. . . . We need buy-in on this, or it will fail."
	  – "Who would be on the school committee? What would their agenda be?"
	  – "Working through departments is one way in which everyone can participate meaningfully in the development of competencies. I also think small groups of faculty meeting in mixed-discipline groups and full faculty discussions should be included in the process."
	• Department-specific competencies are fine, but school-wide ones are not needed:
	  – "School-wide would be redundant with departments and only add busy work and committees."
	  – "We don't need more committees. . . . Keep this work within each department."
	  – "The two-pronged approach shows a lack of trust in departments to do this work."
	  – "The problem of any top-down approach is that we end up with standards that are not rooted in what we actually do in our classrooms."
	• Don't create teacher competencies at all.
	  – "I am skeptical about the exercise even at the department level. I don't see it adding value."
	  – "One of the true richnesses of [Andover] is the fact that we all as teachers bring different competencies to their classroom. Prescribing this will only lead to restricting the ways people teach."

> "The problem of any top-down approach is that we end up with standards that are not rooted in what we actually do in our classrooms."
> —Faculty from round 1

Table 4.4.—continued

Discussion Question	Themes in Faculty Comments
Identifying the roles of instructional coaches and department chairs	

Regarding recommendation 2 to remake the current Evaluation Committee into an instructional coaching committee: Do you support the concept of an instructional coach committee if the coaches were matched by division to the faculty they support—e.g., a STEM faculty person served as a STEM instructional coach?	• Don't have instructional coaches at all:
	  – "I do not support the idea of "a coach committee" because this idea assumes that a group of people always know the best."
	  – "I absolutely do not support the idea of creating instructional coaches. I do not believe we need more mid-level administrators."
	  – Instead of coaches, have teachers observe peers.
	  – Making some teachers into coaches would require expensive and otherwise onerous hiring of temporary or new teacher replacements.
	• Only have instructional coaches if the coaches come from my own discipline.
	• Much more detail is needed to decide whether the coaching would be useful or not:
	  – "I need to know more about the process of evals-frequency, depth, measures before committing to who's best-suited to lead us through it."
	  – "Who would these 'coaches' be? Who would select them?"

Regarding recommendation 3 for instructional coaches rather than department chairs holding annual goal-setting conversations with individual teaching faculty: In your view, what role—e.g., the department chair, a division-specific instructional coach, someone else—would best lead a 30-minute one-on-one goal setting conversation with you each year?	• Department chair is best, shared by assistant department chairs in the larger departments: – "Ideally chairs could do this because they are likely to have a good working relationship with the faculty member, but we ask far too much of chairs already. So one important attraction to an instructional coach, for me, is about alleviating the workload on the chair." • Best yet is a structure for sustained conversations about instruction: • "The most effective changes in my teaching have come from sustained collaborations with colleagues working toward common goals. A couple of meetings with an administrator or chair doesn't really produce meaningful change: it becomes a box to check. Working with someone regularly and consistently provides meaningful and effective support and accountability. What would be helpful would be for administrators to help facilitate the formation of small mixed-discipline groups of colleagues who might be pursuing a common goal that is not discipline-specific." • "Conversations with the course head or colleagues who are teaching the other sections of the same course can be a helpful form of coordination."

Regarding recommendation 8 about who oversees the periodic formal teaching review: Many participants feel that department chairs, not instructional coaches, should oversee the periodic teaching review process. Do you agree? Or does your view change if instructional coaches are matched by division to faculty—e.g., a world languages instructional coach oversees a world language faculty person's formal teaching review?	• The department chair should be in charge of the process:
	  – "The people that need to be involved are the ones that will be providing the support going forward… the people who will be helping me reach my professional goals. That sounds more like a department chair than a 'coach' or colleague observer, who can provide useful feedback and ideas."
	  – "Education is about relationships….the department chair should be cultivating relationships with their department, and that becomes a trusted resource."
	  – Instead of oversight by an administrator, set up peer mentoring to distribute the responsibility and increase conversations about teaching:
	  – "We need consistent teaching buddies who can help provide a mirror to the teacher. I would trust that a colleague who was observed in this way would respond well to feedback offered in a trusting relationship. If we need paperwork, maybe there is a rating scale of some kind where the buddy provides a rating with comments and the observed teacher provides "rebuttal" to any comments offered. Then, that paperwork can flow to the dept chair for review and follow up. Make the process sustainable."

> "The most effective changes in my teaching have come from sustained collaborations with colleagues working toward common goals."
> —Teacher in round 1

Table 4.4.—continued

Discussion Question	Themes in Faculty Comments
Improving the anonymous student survey	

Regarding recommendation 10 about a shorter anonymous school-wide student survey that focuses on minimum expectations for courses: Separate from and in addition to teacher-run surveys of students, RAND recommended in round 1 that Andover revise the anonymous school-wide survey. Specifically, RAND suggested the following: (1) cut the anonymous Qualtrics survey down to 5 minutes, (2) run it in every course in each trimester, (3) add a suggested script at the beginning that draws on prior research to reduce bias in student responses, (4) focus all of the questions on course basics like receipt of a syllabus at the beginning of class, clear course expectations, and clear grading policy rather than higher-order questions about the quality of instruction or liking a teacher, (5) produce automatically generated reports each spring that focuses on the middle—not outlier—ratings to help further mitigate bias. Reading that list of five suggestions, do you have suggestions about the process or the survey content to make an anonymous student survey better?	• A survey about "course basics" is not necessary since administrators would hear about these problems through other channels.
	• Student surveys are too biased to be useful:
	  – "The [Qualtrics] student evaluation has been incredibly unhelpful and quite hurtful to many faculty."
	  – "Students who have not done well in the class will invariably feel that the grading policy is unclear. There are just lots of ways to introduce bias into these questions."
	• A "course basics" survey will damage trust with teachers:
	  – RAND recommendation 10 would be tantamount to "ratemyteacher.com."
	  – "This sounds like surveillance rather than effective management."
	• So long as the items on the school-wide survey are kept as factually oriented as possible, a "course basics" survey would be acceptable.
	  – "Sometimes there are teachers who sometimes do not meet basic expectations. Having data like this is essential to help those teachers overcome deficiencies they might have. We absolutely cannot leave chairs and administrators solely reliant on what they hear from student and parent complaints. Data helps."
	  – "I see this only as a way to put data behind anecdotes. It could either confirm or dispute what is likely already out there."
	  – "It seems like the purpose of this survey would be to establish the lowest, most basic level of teacher competence. I suppose, though, that anecdotal evidence is heavily biased and if a survey like this could counteract that bias, and provide more support to teachers with marginalized identities, I would be in favor."
	  – "I don't think it would be a good idea to ask subjective questions like whether or not the teacher is a 'fair grader' or 'prepared for class' (these open-ended questions invite deeply problematic bias). But I do think asking yes/no questions like 'is the grading policy posted on Canvas' and 'is the teacher on time for class' would be fine. With that said … it's hard for me to imagine this kind of evaluation being used in a way that is supportive for excellent teachers, only punitive for teachers who receive low marks."
	  – "I don't mind if they comment on my punctuality, or knowing them by name, but I don't think they can tell if I'm prepared or assess the timeliness of work returned given the sheer volume that comes in (sometimes 45 x 3–4 page papers in one day)."
	  – "Less is more. A VERY BRIEF student survey about punctuality and other mundane topics is sufficient."
	  – "Let's frame it in terms of whether the course, not the teacher, meets minimum expectations. Dean of Studies office would send out once a term (prior to midterm) a single survey to be administered during advising. Survey would have students' courses pre-filled, and for each they would answer the questions about course basics. Reports are generated promptly every term to surface issues and give teachers a chance to fix them."

> "The [Qualtrics] student evaluation has been incredibly unhelpful and quite hurtful to many faculty."
> —Teacher in round 1

NOTE: All 158 faculty were invited to participate in round 2. 48% of faculty logged in to at least review comments in round 2.

Results from Round 3

Based on the comments and ratings from rounds 1 and 2, we then substantially revised the original recommendations from round 1 for faculty to re-rate in the final and third round. We intentionally did not ask faculty to re-rate any recommendation which they had deemed helpful in round 1. In round 3, we instead posed five consolidated recommendations to which the two most significant revisions were as follows:

- We dropped the idea of instructional coaches because of the widespread negative reaction to the idea and the importance of teacher buy-in to whatever process Andover ultimately adopts. Instead of coaches, we proposed that department chairs continue to run the teaching review process and we then proposed other ways to simplify the evaluation structure given the feedback from interviews and prior ExpertLens rounds about lack of chair and faculty time and a pattern of incomplete execution of the more complex parts of Andover's intended teaching review process.
- We proposed a bottom-up approach to developing the foundational documents (i.e., student competencies and teacher competencies) needed for Andover to build a more coherent instructional system.

In Table 4.5, we show the topics for each recommendation, faculty's median rating of the question "How helpful would this recommendation be for your development as a teacher?" and the ExpertLens determination about the faculty's ratings. The full wording of each potential recommendation and ratings are in Table A.3.

To provide more nuance, Figure 4.1 shows the full distributions of faculty ratings for reach recommendation. The charts show that faculty most strongly endorsed the annual conversations with faculty and the chair-run streamlined formal evaluation every six years. They also endorsed, but less strongly, student competencies and the revised student survey process. They were least positive about identifying desired teachers teaching competencies, where the greatest number of faculty (11) rated it as low as possible and the fewest (4) rated it as high as possible.

Looking at ratings by faculty demographic characteristics (see Table 4.6; we report on participation rates by demographic group in Table 4.2), teachers of color rated the recommendations most positively, endorsing all five recommendations as helpful. White teachers were split (with high and low ratings) about the student

TABLE 4.5

Faculty Ratings from Round 3 About the Helpfulness of a Policy Change for Their Teaching

Potential Recommendation Topic	Median Helpfulness Rating	Faculty Overall Determination
1: Identify desired student competencies, starting in departments and then in an iterative process with a school-wide committee	7	Helpful
2: Identify desired teacher competencies after student competencies and in the same manner	6	Uncertain
3: Hold an annual conversation with each faculty led by department chair	7	Helpful
4: Streamline the formal evaluation process and run it every six years. The chair would lead the process, and the other observers would be removed.	7	Helpful
5: Revise the school-wide student survey and separate out instructional questions into faculty-run surveys	7	Helpful

NOTE: All 158 faculty were invited to rate the five recommendations on a range of 1 to 9, where 1 was "not at all helpful" and 9 was "very helpful." 39 percent of the faculty rated one or more of the recommendations. As described in Appendix A, the faculty overall determination was calculated automatically by an ExpertLens algorithm based on the distribution of teacher ratings, and there were four potential determinations: helpful; uncertain helpfulness; unhelpful; disagreement.

FIGURE 4.1
Distribution of Faculty Ratings from Round 3

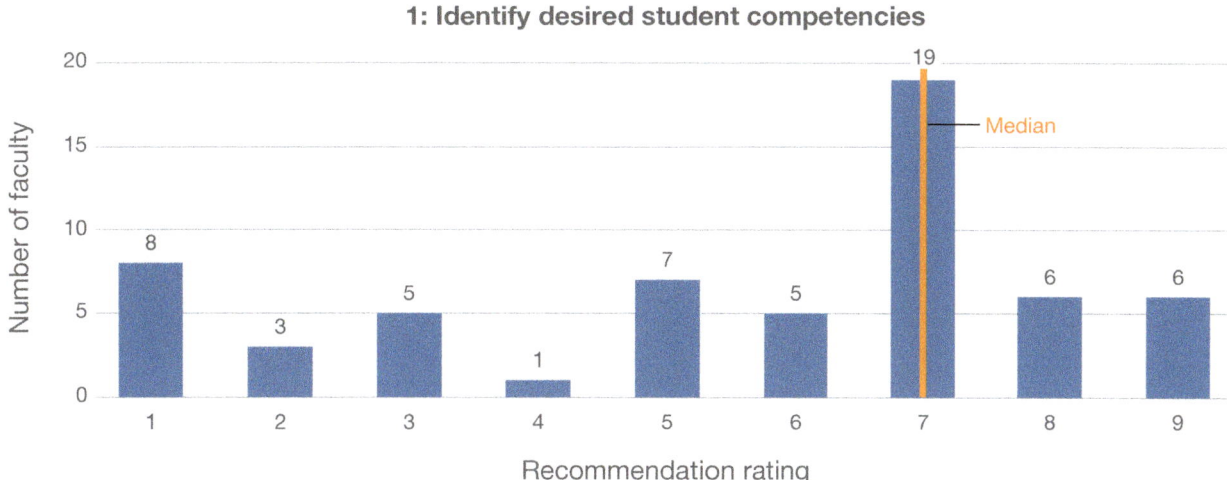

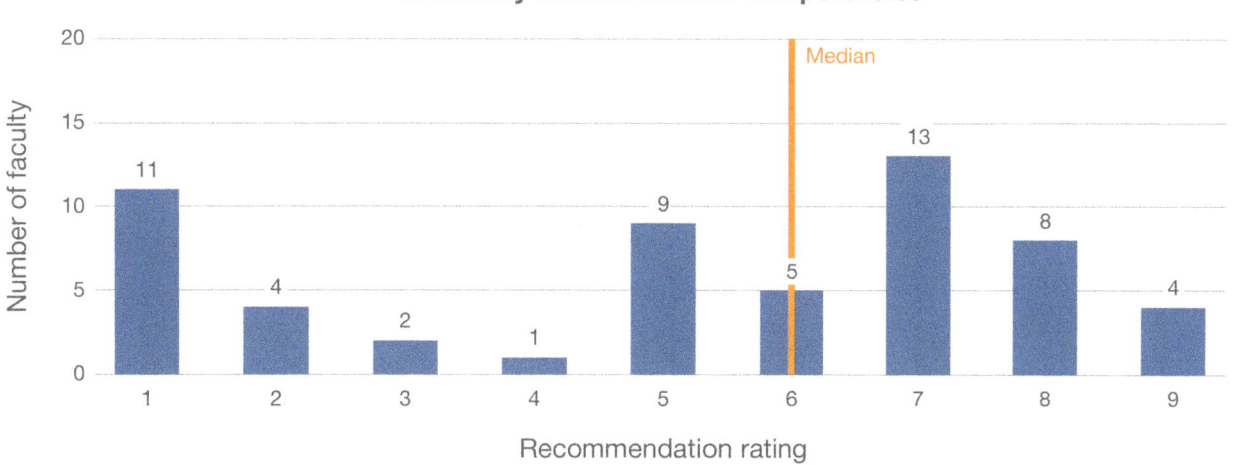

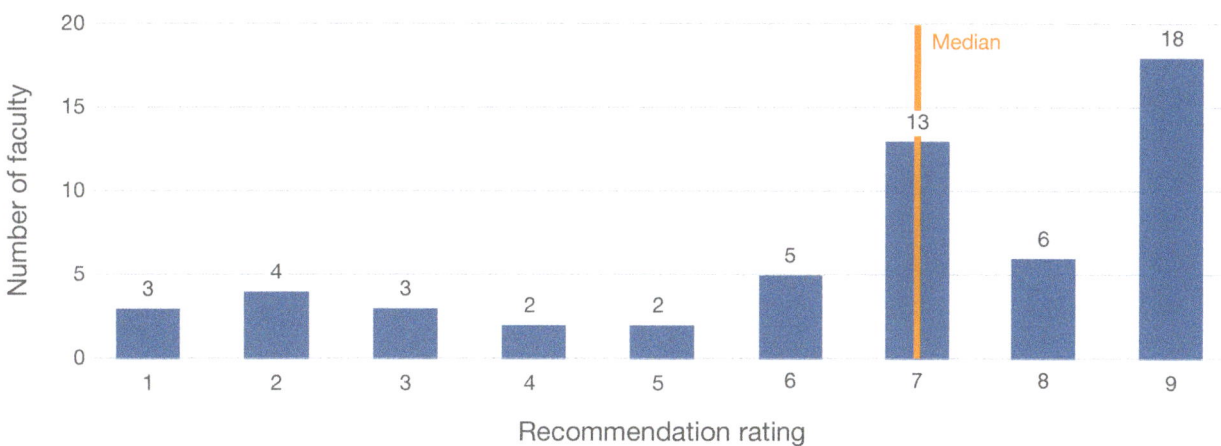

FIGURE 4.1—CONTINUED

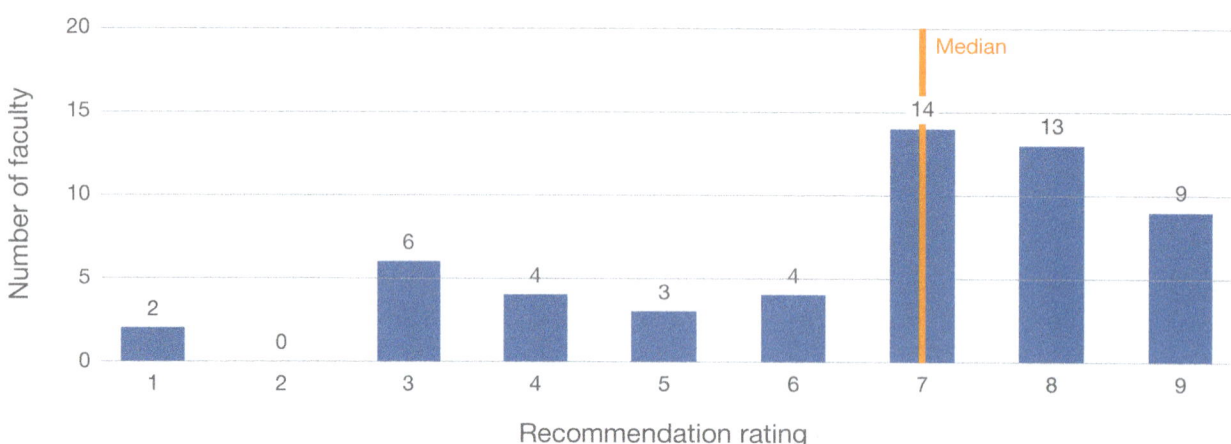

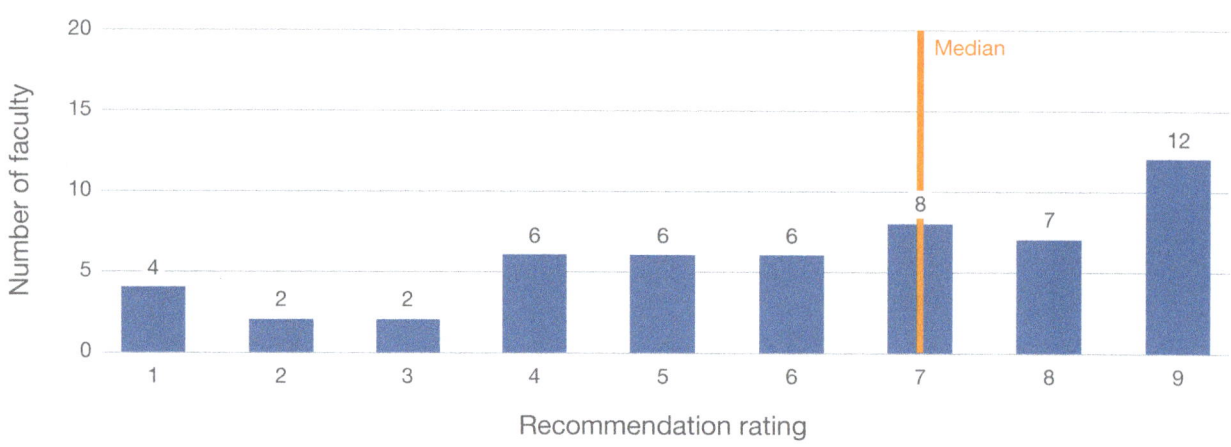

competencies recommendation, were uncertain about the teacher competencies and the student survey recommendations, and endorsed the other two. Faculty with less than ten years of experience rated the recommendations lower than those with ten or more years of experience.

Finally, to provide some of the impetus for the final recommendations we present in Chapter 5, Table 4.7 outlines the themes that emerged from faculty comments in round 3.

TABLE 4.6
Faculty Subgroup Round 3 Determinations and Median Rating About the Helpfulness of a Policy Change for Their Teaching

Recommendation Topic	Overall Determination (median rating)	Teachers of Color	White	Less Than 10 Years	10 or More Years	Female	Male
1: Student competencies	Helpful (7)	Helpful (7)	Disagreement (6)	Uncertain (5)	Helpful (7)	Helpful (7)	Helpful (7)
2: Teacher competencies	Uncertain (6)	Helpful (7)	Uncertain (5)	Uncertain (5.5)	Uncertain (6)	Uncertain (5.5)	Uncertain (6)
3: Annual conversation	Helpful (7)	Helpful (8.5)	Helpful (7)	Helpful (7)	Helpful (7)	Helpful (7)	Helpful (7)
4: Streamlined formal evaluation process	Helpful (7)	Helpful (8)	Helpful (7)	Uncertain (6)	Helpful (7)	Helpful (7)	Helpful (7)
5: Revised student survey	Helpful (7)	Helpful (7.5)	Uncertain (6)	Uncertain (6)	Helpful (7)	Helpful (7)	Helpful (6.5)
Number who rated	60	15	45	19	41	31	29

NOTE: All 158 faculty were invited to rate the 5 recommendations on a range of 1–9, where 1 was "not at all helpful" and 9 was "very helpful." 39% of the invited faculty provided ratings. As described in Appendix A, the faculty overall determination is calculated automatically by an ExpertLens algorithm based on the distribution of teacher ratings, and there are four potential determinations: helpful; uncertain helpfulness; unhelpful; disagreement.

TABLE 4.7
Themes in Faculty Comments from Round 3

Recommendation Topic	Faculty Comments by Low, Middle, and High Ratings
1: Student competencies	• Those who rated it low (1–3) were alternately concerned about its usefulness in practice, creating a "cookie-cutter experience," and the inclusion of social and emotional skills, which they deemed too subjective to measure. • Those in the middle (4–6) expressed some concern about lack of time to create the document, or an overfocus on the listed competencies, but said that the process of naming the competencies could be useful for pedagogy and course planning and getting teachers on the same page. • Those who rated it high (7–9) said that it would help let students know what to expect and would be a necessary first step toward curricular review. They endorsed starting the process in departments.
2: Teacher competencies	• Those who rated it low (1–3) were alternately concerned that competencies would harm the diversity of faculty or add "busywork." Some suggested a need to first create institutional competencies or to use competencies only to hire teachers and then trust them to do their work once at Andover. • Those in the middle (4–6) expressed some concern a lack of time to do them well, a need for faculty themselves to create the list, an allowance for different departments to have different competencies, and a need for professional development afterward so that teachers could develop some competencies. • Those who rated it high (7–9) said that it would be helpful for new teachers but that it needed to allow for creativity.
3: Annual conversation	• Those who rated it low (1–3) said that such conversations should happen organically and not be required, that they should be required only for new or inexperienced teachers, and that the school should not hire a full-time project manager. • Those in the middle (4–6) said that there should be 2, not 1, conversations per year, and felt there should not be a full-time project manager. • Those who rated it high (7–9) said that conversations about goals were the kind of peer-to-peer coaching that would actually be helpful for teachers, and suggested there be guidance for the conversations. Several stressed the necessity of a full-time project manager to make the review process viable, and that this person be connected to the Dean's office rather than Tang.
4: Streamlined formal evaluation process	• Those who rated it low (1–3) said that every six years was too frequent given the time required for formal reviews, or were concerned about the removal of a peer observation and the Evaluation Committee from the formal review. • Those in the middle (4–6) expressed some concern about the removal of the peer observation and the Evaluation Committee from the formal review and some felt there was no additional benefit to doing it every six years rather than every eight. Some advocated for the formal review to be tied to salary decisions. • Those who rated it high (7–9) liked the streamlining of the review, liked department chairs running it, and liked the increased frequency. Some wished to retain more observers in the formal review.
5: Revised student survey	• Those who rated it low (1–3) suggested the school find other ways besides student surveys to surface concerns or issues with courses, were concerned that the survey results would be used to "police" teachers, or said that student surveys were fundamentally too biased to be used. Some said that running a survey before midterms was too early. Others said that that the survey would simply amount to more busywork and that after the school realized the results were not actionable would increase the length of the surveys. • Those in the middle (4–6) cautioned that the survey would be important for professionalism but that administrators needed to handled it with care. Asking students to complete them all at once in advising might encourage students to compare teachers rather than think through the courses. • Those who rated it high (7–9) said that the survey would be a good way to ensure baseline expectations are met and to protect students' ability to report things they don't feel comfortable telling a department chair. But they cautioned that students needed guidance on how to fill it out, and that administrators needed guidance on how to interpret it. They also said the items should align to school policy and be verifiable information. They liked separating out the standardized school-wide survey from faculty-run surveys.

NOTE: All 158 faculty were invited to rate the 5 recommendations on a range of 1–9, where 1 was "not at all helpful" and 9 was "very helpful." 39 percent of faculty rated one or more recommendation.

Summary of the Recommendations Faculty Endorsed

Andover faculty endorsed the eight recommendations, as shown in Table 4.8. They did so either during round 1 or round 3. We draw on these results for our final recommendations, presented in Chapter 5. The results show that, on the whole, the teaching faculty prefer department-specific rather than centralized processes, they welcome self-run student surveys and annual department-led self-studies, they welcome peer observations, and they welcome a more frequent chair-led teaching review. However, their comments also convey concerns about the use and interpretation of information gathered in the teaching review, skepticism about school-wide processes, and a desire to avoid time-consuming processes that would add to their responsibilities.

TABLE 4.8
The Eight Recommendations Andover Teachers Deemed Helpful

Potential Recommendation Topic	Median Helpfulness Rating
1: Have faculty field their own student surveys each year, separate from and in addition to the anonymous school-wide student survey	9
2: Observe at least one class of another faculty member within their department each year	9
3: Identify desired student competencies	7
4: Hold an annual conversation with each faculty led by department chair	7
5: Streamline the formal evaluation process and run it every 6 years. The chair would lead the process, and the other observers would be removed.	7
6: Revise the school-wide student survey and separate out instructional questions into faculty-run surveys	7
7: Write the self-reflection at the end of the teaching review rather than the beginning	7
8: Select a self-study topic each year in each department	7

NOTE: All 158 faculty were invited to rate these recommendations on a range of 1–9, where 1 was "not at all helpful" and 9 was "very helpful." As described in Appendix A, the faculty overall determination was calculated automatically by an ExpertLens algorithm based on the distribution of teacher ratings, and there were four potential determinations: helpful; uncertain helpfulness; unhelpful; disagreement.

CHAPTER 5

Recommendations

In this chapter we present our full, detailed recommendations. The literature review, interviews of administrators from other independent schools, interviews with Andover department chairs, and faculty feedback in ExpertLens inform these recommendations.

Although our recommendations and their evidence base are confined to academic teaching, we believe that the overarching principles we espouse about designing a coherent system, simplifying, and focusing on logistics to ensure full implementation applies to Andover's athletic, residential, and advising reviews as well. We also emphasize that successful institutional change requires faculty buy-in, dedicated time to do the work well, commitment on the part of institutional leaders to provide the time and other resources required, and commitment to designing a simple, sustainable system. Below we organize our detailed recommendations into two high-level recommendations, and we conclude with a table that summarizes the recommendations.

Start a Multi-Year Process to Design a Coherent Instructional System

Andover should develop and initiate a multi-year process plan to align its existing instructional resources and processes into a more coherent instructional system. Such a system starts with desired student competencies, incorporates departmental review activities to ensure instruction is promoting those competencies, and ends with a teaching review process that flows from the desired competencies. Andover should have clearer, and widely shared, learning expectations for students so that teachers know what they are aiming for and what they are expected to do.

This recommendation comports with NEASC's 2022 review for continued accreditation for the "creation of school-wide curriculum and instructional plans" and the 2022 Andover Anti-Racist Taskforce's report, which recommended more operational guidelines for departments and clearer job and review expectations for teachers. Andover has a solid base of past work from which to build, and Andover leaders should draw on existing resources and communicate that this process will recognize past work and maintain a reasonable degree of instructional autonomy.

To that end, **we suggest that Andover start its first year of this process by agreeing upon and articulating the skills and competencies it wishes students to acquire over the course of their time at Andover.** Faculty feedback to RAND indicates that the process by which Andover teachers and administrators approach this process will be of huge importance for faculty buy-in, which research confirms is absolutely central to successful execution. Andover faculty signaled a clear preference that this process start with departments updating, creating, or re-approving their desired student competencies. To achieve greater cohesion and ultimately reach an explicit, school-wide curriculum and instructional plan, divisions could first look across their departments' lists and note discrepancies and overlap among them to develop a division list. Then a school-wide committee (with wide teacher representation) could do the same across the divisions' lists. This would likely necessitate some degree of iterative revisions among departments, divisions, and the school-wide committee to eventually outline a widely shared set of desired student skills and competencies at the school level. Departments' lists could be a more specific expression of a subset of the school-wide skills and competencies, and not every department or even every division's instructional goals need to contribute to every single skill or competency on the school-wide list. Although our scope is academic teaching, the student competencies could be designed to reflect the full range of things Andover wants students to know and do inside and outside the classroom.

In the second year of this process, we suggest that each department, refresh, create, or re-approve its curriculum map. Before the school year starts, the Dean of Studies could provide some guidance and examples, and some department chairs could share in all-staff meeting how they have approached this in the past. This would help generate ideas for departments to consider as they start their self-study. The aim is that faculty take the second year to review their departmental course offerings to ensure that the courses—whether diploma-required or elective—cover the skills and competencies the department is trying to instill and that the courses create a coherent sequence of study that helps students gain the skills they need to progress to higher-level courses and readiness for college. Ideally, this exercise will be the sustained conversation about pedagogy and instruction that Andover faculty members frequently told us was their most rewarding form of professional development. It could involve peer observations within the department for deeper discussions of what different courses' instructional aims could and should be. We suggest that by the end of the year, each department provide a curriculum map to the Dean of Studies and discuss what changes, if any, the department made.

In the third year, we suggest that Andover revise faculty job expectations in the *General Policies Handbook* and the *Faculty and Administrator Supplement to the General Policies Handbook*. Several teachers raised the desire for greater clarity about their job description during the ExpertLens process. The 2022 Anti-Racist Taskforce report also requested that the school revisit and further specify its written job expectations. Here we again suggest that departments first propose updates to these to make the expectations of teachers clearer. After departments propose their suggestions, a school-wide committee could aggregate the suggestions, consider them, and then propose a revision to the relevant sections of the Handbook. The school administration could then work in concert with departments to revise and finalize the list of professional expectations of teachers.

The four dimensions of teaching practice outlined in the *Faculty Evaluation Handbook* could be a starting point for these updates. In keeping with a coherent instructional system, the written job expectations should include that teachers design their courses to cover some of the department's desired student competencies. We also suggest that the written expectations include annual participation in department self-studies, classroom observations of peers, and administration of surveys to students to gather feedback. Further, whatever professional activity is covered in the school-wide student survey (e.g., posting the course syllabus to Canvas by a set time point) should also be included in the written job expectations.

We note that this recommendation to revise the written job expectations for teachers intentionally falls short of the one we proposed in ExpertLens about identifying desired teacher competencies. Ultimately, we feel that Andover need not create a list of desired teacher competencies, because the published evidence from research and the examples we obtained from other independent schools are not sufficiently strong to merit the considerable time required to develop them and to overcome faculty objections to their development. Identifying desired teacher competencies was the most negatively rated proposal we posed to Andover teachers. Many faculty felt that the creation of school-wide teacher competencies would be busywork at best and would unduly impinge on teacher autonomy at worst.

In the fourth year, we suggest that Andover create guidance for the teaching reviews to link them more clearly to the coherent instructional system. For example, Andover should create a guide for annual informal reviews between chairs and teachers that includes a prompt to discuss particular student skills or competencies the teacher is trying to improve. Likewise, the classroom observation protocol that chairs would use during the formal teaching reviews should be revised to link more explicitly to the instructional system, such as by prompting the chair to note which student skills or competencies the class is developing, and, in the post-observation conversation prompting about how the class ties into the larger progression of skills in the course and across courses in the department. The faculty member's self-reflection and the chair's formal review should also situate the faculty member's contributions within the larger departmental sequence of instruction. We suggest that the fourth year for creation of this guidance so that Andover will have the time needed to develop the precursor policies—student competencies, course sequences, and updated teacher job descriptions—needed to structure guidance for the informal and formal teaching reviews.

For the fifth year, we recommend that Andover department chairs and administrators together decide whether to invite external observers (or other departments at Andover) to conduct reviews of each department. By the end of the fourth year, Andover will have developed all elements of a more coherent instructional system. External feedback about that newly aligned system may help departments refine and improve their work. However, we recognize that coordinating external observers can be a time-consuming process. We also did not find conclusive research about external reviews, and Andover faculty rated this potential activity as of "uncertain" helpfulness during the ExpertLens process. We therefore recommend that Andover faculty revisit this idea after the first four years of its work to develop a more coherent instructional system, and to decide whether external observers would be beneficial.

To maintain a coherent instructional system going forward, we suggest that each year departments select a self-study activity. For instance, curriculum mapping would be each department's self-study topic in the second year of the process we propose. But the self-study topic need not be the same for each department in each year thereafter. Our interviews of chairs indicate that faculty members in most departments already engage in some self-study activities, such as developing student assessments, grade norming exercises, and revising a faculty mentoring system within the department. In recognition of time constraints, we suggest that departments select only one study activity for each school year, submit this topic to the Dean of Studies at the outset of the year, and provide a short, written update to the Dean at the end of the year on the outcomes of that activity. Some departments might wish to work together in a self-study to foster inter-disciplinary or divisionwide work. While we recommend that departments identify their own self-study topic, we believe that they should revisit desired student competencies and curriculum mapping every six years, so that each chair would lead these two self-studies once during their term. As a part of the self-study, **we further recommend that each faculty member observe at least one class per year by a fellow teacher in their department.** We suggest this to contribute to building instructional coherence and a culture of ongoing inquiry about instruction that so many faculty endorsed.

Focus on Full Execution of Andover's Ten Guiding Principles for Teaching Reviews, and Simplify Some Processes to Reach That Goal

Andover should retain its ten guiding principles (quoted in Chapter 2) for its teaching review process and modify some of its processes (mostly to simplify them) so as to increase the likelihood that the principles are fully implemented.

Specifically, **we recommend that Andover require all department chairs to hold annual individual conversations of at least 30 minutes with their faculty members**. These would be goal-setting conversations in which teachers and department chairs set goals for the year and discuss ones from the prior year. In this conversation, the faculty member and chair would also discuss what professional development activities the teacher might pursue that year. The goal is for Andover to train its department leaders more effectively and to provide actionable feedback and to create a culture in which teachers set annual teaching goals and seek out and implement feedback.

We recommend that Andover **adopt an online documentation system** and require chairs to take free-form short summary notes of the annual informal teaching reviews, including any professional development recommendations. Both teachers and the relevant chair and administrators would have access to a teacher's account in the system. Documenting annual feedback conversations is a practice recommended in the literature, and it is consistent with Andover's eighth guiding principle. (Folio, for example, has developed a software system designed for independent schools that allows teachers and administrators to manage and document professional development activities. It is designed for tracking requested, approved, and completed professional development, which is often hard for schools to track.) Chairs could also draw on their written summaries from the annual informal reviews when writing a summary of the faculty person during the periodic formal teaching review.

We recognize that annual conversations require a significant time commitment for chairs, especially in large departments. Andover has newly introduced assistant chairs in the largest departments, and we suggest that chairs of these departments share the responsibility with assistant chairs. But we also suggest that chairs receive administrative support to help make these annual conversations happen and that they get some time back in the form of more streamlined formal reviews, which we discuss later in this section. While it is outside the scope of our review, we suggest that Andover consider other ways to reduce chair workload and free up more time for annual informal teaching reviews, periodic formal reviews, and a more robust annual departmental self-study process that we describe in these recommendations.

To provide more administrative support, **we recommend that Andover hire a full-time project manager to oversee Andover's faculty review processes and ensure that reviews happen on time**. While many faculty members stressed the need for more teachers rather than more administrators at Andover, we feel that a project manager is needed to ensure that the core elements of a performance review system occur regularly. Most of the independent schools we interviewed employ a project manager/coordinator to play this role, and it would reduce the administrative burden on chairs. Specifically, this person could coordinate each year with departments' administrative assistants to ensure that they schedule the annual conversations (a time-consuming process that the chairs should not be doing themselves). The project coordinator should also be Andover's point of contact for the online documentation system and should follow up with chairs and teachers to ensure that they add their notes from the annual informal reviews as well as documents for formal reviews. The coordinator would notify chairs and teachers when teachers are due for the periodic formal reviews, and the coordinator would make sure that each person gets the relevant guidance and training for the process at the necessary times. Finally, this coordinator could oversee the logistics of the annual school-wide student survey.

We recommend that Andover retain its chair-led formal review of teachers, but we recommend that it occur every six years throughout a teacher's career, rather than every eight. We also recommend that Andover continue to start these formal reviews as of a teacher's third year at Andover. We acknowledge that the literature does not provide clear guidance about optimal frequency of these formal reviews, but we feel that eight years is too infrequent. Faculty largely endorsed a six-year frequency in the ExpertLens process, and we believe that this is logical, as it coincides with a department chair's tenure. A six-year frequency means that a department chair would, at most, formally review any one faculty member once. While we had considered a more frequent schedule (e.g., every three years), faculty said in ExpertLens that three years was too often. Since the annual informal reviews would be the main vehicle for ongoing conversations about instruction and instructional coherence anyway, we feel that a formal review every six years is sufficient, given annual conversations and a faculty preference for the formal reviews to remain relatively infrequent.

To encourage easier implementation, **we recommend that Andover simplify both its annual informal reviews and its periodic formal ones**. Most of the complexity that we recommend Andover pare back stems from its guiding principle to include multiple measures of performance in teacher review. While research strongly concurs about the use of multiple measures, we believe there are ways to continue the valid practice while still simplifying the review process and reducing time burden.:

1. Eliminate the Annual Performance Review Form. The form has not been used dependably, and we advise instead that chairs type free-form notes during annual 30-minute goal-setting conversations into the online documentation system. While we support the concept of faculty selecting one professional growth activity per year (e.g., Ped Pods, peer observation, video recording and reflection) as stipulated in the Annual Performance Review Form, we feel it is impractical because it is administratively burdensome to monitor.
2. While the specifics are outside our scope, we also recommend simplifying and streamlining the residential, advising, and athletic reviews that are a part of the formal reviews to make the process less time-consuming and easier to enact.
3. Reduce the time required for the periodic formal academic teaching review, which chairs say takes them five to 12 hours per faculty member. The two peer observations and three evaluation committee member observations (in addition to the one observation by the department or division chair) take the most time. We suggest dropping the Evaluation Committee observations altogether and shifting the peer observation out of the formal teaching review into departmental self-studies. Each faculty member would observe at least one class per year taught by a fellow faculty member in their department as part of the annual self-studies.

    We certainly condone classroom observations. In fact, faculty felt that peer observation was some of the best professional development they get. But, observations are time-consuming and difficult to schedule, and it would require substantial additional time and resources to provide the amount of training needed to minimize bias and meet best practices if observations were to continue being part of the formal teaching review system. We therefore recommend eliminating all but the chair's observation from the formal teaching review as one place where Andover can simplify its process and reduce faculty workload. Our suggested shift of peer observations out of the periodic review and into annual department self-studies would actually increase the frequency of peer observations, but place them within what we believe is appropriately a less-formal activity for which peer observers need not receive extensive training. Meanwhile, the Evaluation Committee is a valuable place for needed cross-disciplinary instructional work at the school, and we suggest that the committee could instead reorient to support school-wide work on curriculum and student competencies.
4. Add teacher-introduced classroom artifact(s) and/or lesson plans as one of the multiple measures in a formal review. In the spirit of organizing the formal review around substantive discussion of instruction and pedagogy (rather than checking boxes on a form as Andover teachers told us in ExpertLens they understandably wish to avoid), teachers could accompany their written reflection with examples of student work, lesson plans, or results from one of the faculty's student surveys to illustrate an instructional activity or exercise that follows from one of the teacher's goals.

If these changes were adopted, a teacher's formal review would consist of the following academic elements (in addition to ones the school opts to include for athletics, residential, and advising):

- the department chair's observation of one class during the formal review year accompanied by a pre- and post-observation conversation with the teacher
- the teacher's self-reflection written during the formal review year

- the teacher-provided artifacts from one or more classes that illustrate instructional activity in service of one of the teacher's goals
- the chair's performance review form written at the end of the formal review, which would also draw on notes from the previous years' annual conversations.

We also recommend that Andover revamp the school-wide student survey and remove it from the periodic formal teaching review altogether. To collect developmental feedback for informing instruction we suggest that faculty run their own surveys each year in which they pose instructional questions of their own choosing. Many faculty already do this successfully. Separate from these faculty-run surveys, Andover should significantly revise the anonymous student survey to serve a managerial purpose by informing teachers and the administration whether basic course functions are occurring as intended in each class and providing them the results quickly enough to rectify any problems. If the administration identifies recurring concerns, it would address those directly with the teacher on a more accelerated timeline than the periodic formal review allows.

To create this managerial survey, we recommend that Andover change the current student survey administered in Qualtrics as follows:

- Cut the anonymous survey down to 5 minutes or less. Five minutes equates to approximately 30 simply-structured questions (at a rate of six questions per minute).
- Invite students via a message from the administration to fill out a survey for each course in each trimester.
- Have students take these short course surveys during an advising period.
- Administer the survey prior to midterms so that student input can be acted on while the class is still in session and to mitigate the concern that student ratings are influenced by course grades.
- Restrict the questions to factually oriented ones that are part of the school's expectations for professionalism—for example, that faculty provide students with a syllabi at the beginning of each term, that faculty provide feedback on student work within a timeframe specified in the survey (e.g., one week), that faculty are on time to class. The research suggests that administrators should not ask questions that they can reasonably obtain answers to elsewhere; for example, if Andover has an expectation that faculty should post the course syllabi to Canvas by a set time in the trimester, then Andover should have a separate (and ideally automated) process to directly check for compliance rather than ask students about it. There should be no questions on this school-wide survey about such high-inference concepts as quality of instruction or fairness of grading. Research indicates there are greater concerns about bias in student responses in these types of questions.
- At the beginning of the survey, add a script addressed to students that draws on prior research to reduce bias—particularly bias based on race or gender—in student responses. We provide an example in Chapter 4.
- Andover administrators and faculty should together develop clear guidance regarding how the survey data are interpreted and used, with special consideration of how to interpret negative outlier responses and discuss those responses with the faculty member.
- After each survey, the newly hired project manager should disseminate automatically generated reports to faculty and chairs. The department chair would follow the guidance for interpreting results and discuss any issues that arise with the faculty person.

Finally, we recommend more substantial, more consistent training for all faculty about departmental and teaching review policies, with more intensive training for department chairs. As Andover updates its departmental and teaching review practices and associated policies, Andover leaders should communicate these changes to faculty through multiple methods (e.g., email announcements, faculty meetings, onboarding processes for new instructors). We also recommend that department chairs, as the owners and leaders of many of these new practices, participate in a more comprehensive training that would apprise them of their responsibilities. They should have the opportunity to train in the use of the classroom observation form, model and then practice annual informal feedback conversations; become acquainted with the institutional resources at their disposal; outline the roles of the project manager, chair, and department administrator in enacting informal and formal teaching reviews; and seek support from more-experienced chairs.

Table 5.1 puts our recommendations alongside the current status of departmental and teaching review policy at Andover.

TABLE 5.1
Summary of Andover's Current Policies and RAND's Recommendations

Activity	Current Status	Recommendation
Departmental reviews	Andover encourages departmental reviews but does not have any formal guidance or requirements about them.	• Andover should require that each department engage in a self-study each year. • Departments can be the engine for a multi-year process in which Andover creates a more coherent instructional system. • Every six years, each department should revisit its desired student competencies and its curriculum map. • Each year, each department should discuss the self-study topic with the Dean of Studies and report at the end of the year about the outcomes. • As a part of self-studies, each faculty should observe at least one class of a faculty person within their department each year.

Teaching review	• Chairs are to meet each year with faculty to conduct an informal review, but this largely does not happen.
	• Formal reviews occur in the third and eighth year of a teacher's tenure at Andover, then every eight years thereafter. Department chairs lead the formal reviews.
	• The teaching review process is guided by eight principles.
	• The teaching review theoretically includes the school-wide student survey, but the results are largely not used.
		• The teaching reviews should be one element of a coherent instructional system that starts with departments and the school identifying desired student competencies.
		• Andover should keep its eight guiding principles, enforce them, and retain a department-chair led teaching review process.
		  – Specifically, chairs or assistant chairs should meet with each faculty for at least 30 minutes each year.
		  – Andover should simplify its processes to make them easier to implement.
		  – Also to reduce burden, Andover should retain only the department chair observation within the formal teaching review and drop the Evaluation Committee and peer review observations.
		  – Add teacher-introduced classroom artifact(s) and/or lesson plans as one of the multiple measures in the formal review.
		• Andover should eliminate or replace its teaching review forms and instead adopt an online documentation system to which both the teacher and department chair have access.
		• Andover should hire a project manager to ensure that the informal and formal teaching reviews occur as intended and to reduce burden on chairs in particular.
		• Andover should provide training to teachers and more extended training to chairs about enacting the teaching review.

In conclusion, we reiterate four key lessons from the implementation literature that are essential for institutional change and for making a coherent instructional system work in practice:

- Teacher buy-in is essential to successful change and can be promoted by taking a collaborative approach in which employees are involved in the design of new systems and processes; adopting an iterative approach in which ideas are generated using both bottom-up and top-down approaches, tested in pilot projects, and adopted in phases; and clearly communicating changes and change efforts through multiple channels.
- Institutional commitment is key and can promote faculty buy-in. Institutional commitment can include strong leadership, resources (such as course relief, or other sources of time) to accomplish the work, compensation for additional work, and administrative or project management resources.
- Faculty and departments require time to meet and collate existing resources, develop student competencies, and engage in departmental review activities. Providing adequate time for meaningful collaboration will recognize that some faculty members perceive it as an additional obligation in an already busy schedule. This approach strengthens professional ties and faculty buy-in. In addition, Andover might consider what other administrative tasks department chairs could delegate to an administrative support person.
- Complexity lowers the likelihood of implementation. A simple process entails tools that are relatively easy to learn and use in practice, and that require a reasonable and therefore sustainable time commitment from department chairs and faculty—ideally no more than a couple of hours per faculty member receiving a review. The more complex a review process is, the less likely it is that it will produce the desired outcomes. Although even the simplest systems require up-front time commitments, once a routine is in place, the amount of time needed to maintain the system should reduce over time.

In our view, the main challenge for Andover will be to balance teacher autonomy with sufficient structure to ensure that teachers' lessons and courses build year-on-year in a coherent and comprehensive fashion, such that the courses students take and the instruction they receive over the course of (up to) four years cover Andover's full set of desired learning objectives. There is a strong foundation from which to build. Andover faculty are eager to engage in conversations within their departments about instruction. Some departments have already created a list of desired student competencies and mapped their courses to create coherent course progressions and consistency among different sections of a course. The school's principles for teaching evaluation are supported by research. Taken together, the school can draw on these strengths to develop a robust, coherent instructional system that will benefit students and faculty alike.

CHAPTER 6

Andover's Reactions to the Recommendations

Note to the reader: The Deputy Head of School for Academics and Student Affairs, The Dean of Faculty, and the Chief of Staff at Andover wrote this chapter. The two reviewers of the rest of the report did not review it because it is not a part of RAND's research.

In the past year, the need for a clearer and more coherent curriculum plan and review has been strongly emphasized in reports by NEASC (recommendation #1), Andover's Anti-Racism Task Force, and Andover's Working Group on Assessment and Grading. We are grateful for RAND's work to produce a large literature review about teacher and department reviews, interview current and former department chairs, learn from other independent-school models, survey the Andover faculty in a three-stage process to gain feedback about our context, and ultimately provide recommendations to improve our teaching review process. Not surprisingly, there is a great deal of alignment among recommendations from these various internal and external reports. In this section, we respond to RAND's recommendations.

While we have an excellent academic program as noted by various external and internal reports, we agree that having a more coherent instructional system will provide greater clarity and transparency to all stakeholders to understand the breadth, depth, and complexity of our academic program. Guided by our Statement of Purpose, our values, and our vision of the academic program (see Appendix B), we will ensure that all students and families better understand our academic priorities and expectations.

Andover affirms the following recommendations from RAND:

- The key components of a coherent instructional system include:
  - a clear identification of student skills and knowledge (i.e., competencies) that curricula should cover
  - use of curricula that covers the desired competencies
  - teachers' use of assessments that are aligned to the curriculum
  - professional learning for teachers that covers the curriculum and the desired student skills and knowledge
  - a teaching review that gauges whether teachers use the common instructional framework (i.e., desired student skills and knowledge and teacher competencies) in their courses.
- To make a coherent instructional system work in practice, we need to:
  - Gain teacher buy-in, which is essential to successful change
  - Give faculty and departments time to meet
  - Demonstrate institutional commitment
  - Create a system that is simple enough to execute. Complexity lowers the likelihood of implementation.

We are at different stages of enacting this work to (1) identify student competencies, (2) revise our faculty review process, and (3) establish a department review process. As of fall 2022, we are building on previous curriculum work at the department level and with our Academic Council (department chairs and other academic leaders) to identify observable and transferable student competencies by the end of the 2022–2023 school year. We have also established a faculty task force to review our current faculty evaluation model and propose new ideas based on work previously completed and new information found in this report. We will formalize a new department review process by the end of the 2022–2023 school year. We describe each of these initiatives more fully below.

Student Competencies

We agree that that the first step in moving toward a more coherent instructional system is to identify desired student competencies. Our plan is for departments to identify competencies in fall and winter terms of the 2022–2023 year and then to review them as a full faculty to create a school-wide set of competencies. It was clear through RAND's survey that our faculty favors starting this work at the department level and rather than at a more central level. We still believe, however, that defining competencies at both a department level and in other ways at a school-wide level is fundamental.

There already exists a strong foundation from which to define student competencies within our curriculum. In fact, most departments have created a list of student competencies and have mapped their courses to create coherent vertical course progressions and horizontal consistency among different sections of graduation required courses. Still, Andover has 18 academic departments of various sizes, and we will develop a process to identify and define student competencies that are observable and transferable.

We agree with RAND's recommendation that department chairs should lead this process and will require support in order to do so. During the 2022–2023 school year, we are working with Nicole Furlonge, Professor and Director of the Klingenstein Center at Teachers College, Columbia University, and her team to provide guidance and support for academic departments to articulate student competencies. We have set aside two full days in the fall 2022 term and another two full days in the winter 2023 term for departments to develop student competencies, and we have identified resources within and outside the Academy to support department chairs. In the spring term, we plan to analyze department academic competencies, identify areas of overlap, make connections to school mission and values, and develop recommendations for next steps.

Here are the key questions we are using to guide our work with Nicole Furlonge and her team during fall and winter terms in 2022–2023:

- As we define and document student outcomes within our curriculum, what is a student competency?
- As we build a coherent instructional system, why is the process of developing competencies an important step to fulfill a school's vision for learning?
- What type of framework will be necessary and supportive for department chairs to lead their faculty to define student competencies that are actionable, clear and measurable?
- What elements of a general framework are needed to subsequently review department competencies across the curriculum?
- Once each department has identified and explained their set of competencies, what competencies overlap?
- How do the department competencies align with Andover's academic vision statement as well as the school's statement of purpose and statement of values?

RAND recommends that, in year two, we move toward a curriculum mapping exercise within each department; however, we are not sure if this is how Andover will progress. After we have identified student competencies by department, we may decide that our collective focus will first move instead toward assessment and grading; integrating diversity, equity, inclusion and justice into the curriculum; or other school-wide priorities. At the same time, we will discuss teacher competencies as ways to achieve stated student outcomes within the curriculum. Academic Council, led by the Dean of Studies, will determine how best to build on the student competencies work.

Identifying student competencies this year is an important step in how we develop a revised system for teacher reviews as well as department reviews.

Teaching Reviews

We will revise our teaching review process in a manner that is generally consistent with RAND's recommendations. To lead this work, we have created a Faculty Review Task Force composed of former faculty evaluation committee members and other faculty. During the 2022–2023 academic year, the group will guide further consideration of the RAND recommendations and then develop a revised faculty review system to be approved by the spring of 2023 and implemented beginning in the fall of 2023.

We are pleased by RAND's assessment that our "current teaching evaluation system is sound in its principles and consistent with prior research," and we concur with the criticism that not all of our "existing evaluation policies are implemented consistently and the most complex parts of [our] current teaching review are the ones least likely to be implemented."

We appreciate especially RAND's affirmation of the ten guiding principles our faculty adopted in 2017 for the current faculty evaluation system, which we reprint here in Box 6.1.

We also appreciate and gratefully accept RAND's operational recommendations, which will help us to streamline our review process and ensure that the revised system runs "fully and well" such that it has a

---

BOX 6.1
Andover's Ten Guiding Principles for Our Teaching Review

1. Faculty evaluation will be founded on and guided by the philosophy that the primary purpose of the process is to provide an opportunity for professional growth and development.
2. The basis for evaluation will be clear, written job expectations, as outlined in a job description and/or as outlined in the *General Policies Handbook* and the *Faculty and Administrator Supplement to the General Policies Handbook*.
3. Evaluation procedures will operate in accordance with the non-discrimination policy and apply consistently to all teaching faculty and administrative faculty.
4. The evaluation system will employ the use of multiple measures to assess performance.
5. The evaluation system will be based on established, well-respected research and best practices.
6. The evaluation system will acknowledge the existence of biases, both intentional and unintentional, and include measures to address such biases.
7. Evaluators will have training, specific guidelines and support.
8. Faculty will be evaluated on schedule, balancing the need for regular feedback and a sustainable process.
9. Faculty members will have access to all summary materials included in their evaluation file and have recourse for appeal.
10. The evaluation system will be reviewed at least every eight years.

dependable, substantial positive impact on the ongoing development of our faculty. Like the RAND team, we see the value in such prospective changes as:

- requiring scheduled and more formalized annual conversations between department chairs and individual faculty for the purpose of setting goals, etc.
- retaining the chair-led formal review of teachers but increasing the frequency of such reviews from every eight years to every six years
- redesigning the school-wide student survey
- introducing "classroom artifacts and/or lesson plans" into the review process
- building an online documentation system
- hiring a project manager to oversee the faculty review process (as well as the department review and curriculum review processes) and to support department chairs and other participants
- clarifying expectations and improving training for everyone involved with the faculty review process.

The members of the Faculty Review Task Force, as well as the department chairs and others who build the Department Review system, will bear in mind RAND's wise reminders of the necessity of teacher buy-in, adequate time for meaningful collaboration, institutional commitment, and simplicity of process. This work could also provide context and a lens for which we will research and examine the other components of our operating model, including residential life and athletics.

Department Reviews

This year the Dean of Studies, along with Academic Council, will review RAND's recommendations and determine a process for department reviews – both annual reviews and more formal, comprehensive reviews every few years. Recommendations that faculty endorsed in the RAND surveys included commitments to hold an annual professional development conversation with each faculty member led by the department chair, select a self-study topic each year in each department, and observe at least one class of another faculty member within their department each year. Other ideas to consider will include aligning department priorities with school initiatives, conducting a periodic external review, and supporting different types of professional development for department faculty.

We are committed to having department reviews on a regular rotation. Although every department engages in discussions about teaching and learning, much of the work has been at the multi-section course level with graduation requirements. Our department sizes range from 2 to over 30 faculty, and we have 18 departments. In the past, while the focus of department discussions has centered on excellent teaching and learning at the course level, we have not coordinated a comprehensive department review process well. This is largely because each of our department chairs have six-year terms, have not had time to conduct a full department review, and have not been trained how to do a review well. Engaging with the student competencies work this year will also help each department determine ways to evaluate student outcomes, consider curricular changes, and see how their work connects with other parts of the curriculum.

We agree with RAND that two processes will support both the annual reviews and a more comprehensive review: the self-study activity and having faculty observe classes. The self-study activity will help each department focus on a limited number of goals (one or two) every year. These goals will be determined by the department chair in consultation with their faculty and the Dean of Studies. There will be documentation of progress and discussions about how those goals connect with other parts of the curriculum and school life. Developing an expectation and structure for faculty to observe classes will also promote discussions about teaching and learning. We have yet to determine how many classes a faculty member would observe during a year and what the guidelines will be for those observations.

During a more formal department review process every few years, faculty will need time to meet to identify areas of strength and growth for their department. One approach would be for a department to start this work in the spring term, have a department retreat for two or three days at the end of the school year, assign a small group to work for a week in the summer, and then provide workload relief for one or two members of the department to complete the review with the department chair and together write a report in the fall and winter terms. Support for this work will come from the Dean of Studies office as well as the Tang Institute. Key collaborators will be the Dean of Studies, Dean of Faculty, Assistant Head of School for Analytic Support & Assessment, and Associate Head of School for Equity, Inclusion and Wellness. We will also seek administrative support to help department chairs manage the process, especially with an external group of observers.

We expect that the outcomes of a comprehensive department review would include a clearer understanding of how a department is progressing toward its goals (department and institutional), substantial feedback from external observers, and a strategic direction to guide the department for the next five years.

Looking to our work ahead, faculty will continue to discuss, collaborate, and update department and school-wide principles to guide their teaching. Our work will lead us into discussions about assessment and grading, appropriate professional development, and how our curriculum reflects the school's Statement of Purpose and Statement of Values. As we move toward a whole curriculum review within the next few years, having more explicit systems in place will help us to understand what we are doing well and what we need to improve upon. As a learning community, supporting faculty growth will be central to all this work. RAND's series of specific recommendations gives us sound ideas and reasonable paths to enhance our current practices.

APPENDIX A

Methods

In this technical appendix, we include additional details about the data, methodology, and limitations of our analyses. We describe our literature review, review of Andover documentation, interviews with Andover department chairs, interviews with other independent school administrators and consortia, and use of Expert Lens. We also describe our analytic methods. We used standard qualitative methods to develop our interview protocol and to collect and analyze our interview data. Therefore, this report includes recycled text from other reports that used similar methods (Doan et al., 2022; Wang et al., 2021).

Literature Review

General Parameters for Our Literature Review

This review summarizes research from the K–12 public school systems, higher education, and independent school literature. The topics we chose to include (e.g., curriculum mapping, student competencies, classroom observations) were informed by our conversations with Andover personnel and our previous research related to instructional systems for teaching and learning. Because the published research from independent high schools is sparse, we conducted 12 interviews with leaders of independent schools or organizations that support independent schools to illuminate how Andover's peer organizations are navigating the topics we chose to include. Where gaps in the K–16 research remained, we consulted literature from other sectors, including health care and public-sector performance management systems, based on expert recommendations from colleagues.

As we explain below, the methods we used to review and summarize the literature depended on the volume of research available for each topic we explored. In general, we prioritized literature published since 2000, meta-analyses wherever available, and only those elements of teaching and learning systems that are relevant to Andover. For example, we do not summarize the literature on measuring public school teachers' value add to students' standardized test scores, as that is not a metric under consideration for Andover. Where appropriate—or in cases where we found minimal evidence—we included relevant information or examples from the grey literature, including technical documents or guidance from accreditation organizations and Universities.

Methods to Identify Relevant Literature from K–12 Public Schools

Much of the literature related to effective systems for teaching and learning in K–12 public schools has been informed by or undertaken in response to the Bill & Melinda Gates Foundation's seminal 3-part Measures of Effective Teaching (MET) series. We therefore reviewed this literature to identify key search terms and seminal works specific to teacher observations and student surveys. Next, we conducted an online search of peer-reviewed literature using Google Scholar and the Education Resources Information Center (ERIC) with and without the term *meta-analysis* with terms such as *teacher evaluations, teacher observations, observation rubrics, student surveys, teacher portfolios, evaluator bias, survey bias,* and *validity/reliability of observations,* to identify relevant articles.

Then, we conducted targeted searches using ERIC and Google Scholar to identify literature on the specific components of teaching review systems and professional learning that were most of interest to Andover. These components were *professional learning* (as it relates to teaching reviews), *peer observations, grade norming, instructional coaching,* and *external reviews.* We used search terms that corresponded to these topics. We conducted all our searches iteratively by expanding our search terms to include related relevant topics as they emerged from the articles we reviewed. We also identified additional articles of interest by reviewing the bibliographies of the articles we found during our initial searches.

We prioritized articles published after 2000. After prescreening articles for content, we uploaded articles into Endnote for further review by category (teacher evaluation, student feedback, collaborative professional learning, coaching and feedback, grade norming, student competencies, peer review/observation). Where there was substantial overlap with the postsecondary literature, or where we were unable to identify literature from K–12 sources related to topics that Andover prioritized, we augmented our searches with literature from postsecondary sources (see below). In total, we flagged 347 articles for further review. Of these 347 articles, we discarded 186 based on their lack of relevance to the Andover context.

In our review of the articles related to teaching reviews and student feedback, we prioritized articles written after 2015 that described general principles for effective teacher observations and use of student surveys, believing these to be most relevant to the post Every Student Succeeds Act context. We abstracted relevant information about promising practices and common approaches from these articles into a spreadsheet organized by topic (e.g., choosing an observation or student feedback instrument, getting teacher buy-in, training users, implementation, and minimizing bias). The information on this spreadsheet formed the basis of our initial draft on these sections, which we augmented with literature from our iterative searches throughout the drafting phase.

Methods to Identify Relevant Literature from Higher Education

To find relevant literature from higher education, we distilled a list of initial search terms from our categories of interest (e.g., curriculum review, curriculum mapping, peer review, collaborative peer learning, program learning outcomes, and student feedback). Using these initial search terms, with and without the term "meta-analysis", we conducted a search in Google Scholar and ERIC per topic to identify (1) relevant articles, (2) additional search terms, and (3) additional citations of interest. We repeated this process until we reached saturation. In cases where literature was sparse or we were unable to identify evidence of best practices, we searched the grey literature for technical documents produced by regional accreditation organizations and institutions of higher education in the United States to identify accepted practices.

After prescreening articles for content, we uploaded relevant articles into Endnote for further review. During our review, we prioritized articles that were generalizable to secondary contexts. We abstracted relevant information about promising practices or common approaches by category into a spreadsheet organized by topic (e.g., definition of practice, implementing practice, and enabling conditions for practice). As with the K–12 literature, the information we abstracted formed the basis of our original draft on these sections; however, we augmented this information with additional literature from our iterative searches throughout the drafting phase.

Methods to Identify Literatures/Tools About Independent Schools

To identify teaching review processes in independent schools, we started by an online search of peer-reviewed literature using Google Scholar and ERIC. In our searches, we used the terms *private school* or *independent school* to focus our search on independent schools. Our searches also included terms such as *teacher evaluation*, *teaching review*, *evaluation system*, *classroom observation*, and *student feedback*. Database searches for teacher evaluation always included teacher and evaluation: variations for teacher included educator, instructor, and faculty; variations for evaluation included appraisal, self-review, assessment. Occasionally, we added *practices* or *methods* after *teacher evaluation* to refine search for tools (especially when searching for guides and when searching independent school networks for handbooks). We then searched websites of independent school networks (National Association of Independent Schools, NEASC, Accrediting Commission for Community and Precollegiate Arts Schools, Association of Independent Schools in New England, Association of Waldorf Schools of North America, The Association of Boarding Schools, Association of Independent Schools of Greater Washington) for tools, materials, or forms related to classroom observation, student feedback, and teacher evaluation.

Andover Document Review

We asked Andover leaders and department chairs to provide us with documents relevant to our understanding of Andover's teaching and departmental review processes. Examples of documents provided by Andover leadership included the *Faculty Evaluation Handbook*, course schedule, Faculty Evaluation Committee reports, teaching competencies, teaching review forms and templates (e.g., student feedback form, faculty self-reflection template; annual review form) and NAESC accreditation reports and recommendations. Examples of documents provided by Andover department chairs included department-developed student surveys, self-reflection forms, guidance for incorporating instructional feedback into teaching practices, and department faculty handbooks. We reviewed these documents to inform our understanding of the Andover context and the teaching and departmental review processes and practices.

Andover Department Chair Interviews

During the months of October–November 2021, the two project leaders from RAND individually interviewed all current chairs and all former chairs for those departments where the current chairs had started their term in 2019–2020 or later. We included former chairs in these instances because Andover had suspended its normal teaching review practices due to the pandemic. In all, RAND interviewed 28 current or former chairs, of which 11 had started as chair in 2019–2020 or later. All Andover departments and divisions were represented among our interviewees.

We conducted one-hour telephone interviews with 28 current or former department chairs at Andover in the fall of 2021. The purpose of the interviews was to gather information about implementation of the teaching review and departmental review processes that were in place at Andover. We included former department chairs if the current chair started their term in the 2019–2020 school year or later. Andover suspended its teaching and department review processes in spring 2020, at the beginning of the COVID-19 pandemic. Thus, department chairs who began their terms in the 2019–2020 school year had less experience with the process than chairs who had been in the position longer. At the beginning of the COVID-19 pandemic in March 2020; a majority of the current department chairs began their terms after the start of the pandemic. All Andover departments and divisions were represented among our interviewees.

We interviewed ten current "old" chairs, seven former chairs, and 11 new chairs, for a 100 percent response rate, as shown in Table A.1. We also separately interviewed the six of the nine members of the faculty evaluation committee to gain insight into the role and responsibilities of the committee and the evolution of the teaching review process at Andover.

TABLE A.1
Andover Department Chair Interviewees

Department or Division	Current "Old" Chair	Former Chair	Current New Chair	Total
Archaeology Department	1			1
Art Department	1			1
English Department		1	1	2
History and Social Science Department		1	1	2
Mathematics Department		1	2	3
Music Department		1	1	2
Natural Sciences Division	1	1	2	4
Philosophy and Religious Studies Department		1	1	2
Physical Education	1			1
Theatre and Dance Department			1	1
World Languages Division	6	1	2	9

NOTE: Current chairs began their six-year term as chair before the 2019–2020 school year and were still in the role at the time of our interview. Former chairs ended their six-year term before the 2019–2020 school year and new chairs began their term in the 2019–2020 school year. At Andover, some smaller departments (e.g., with one or two faculty) are grouped into divisions. The Natural Sciences Division includes Biology, Chemistry and Physics; the World Languages Division includes Chinese, Classics, Greek, Latin, French, German, Japanese, Russian, and Spanish. The mathematics department has two co-chairs.

The 28 chairs we interviewed were veterans of Andover; they had taught at the school for an average of 14 years, with years of Andover experience ranging from four to 28. Twenty-one of the 28 interviewees had ten or more years of experience teaching at Andover. The departments they led ranged in size from as few as one instructor (i.e., the chair) in some language departments to as many as 30.[1] The three largest departments—Mathematics, English, and History—each had more than ten faculty.

The one-hour interviews followed a semi-structured protocol and included topics pertinent to teaching and departmental reviews, such as the annual student survey, the annual informal review, the periodic formal reviews, and departmental review activities. We asked chairs to describe what elements of the teaching review were and were not enacted in practice, how the activities that were enacted worked in practice, and which elements of the teaching review did and did not work well.

---

[1] This count excludes teaching fellows and adjuncts. Most departments had none, and the largest had as many as five.

Interviews with Independent School Administrators and Independent School Service Organizations

We conducted one-hour telephone interviews with administrators at eight independent schools and four staff at independent school service organizations in fall 2021 and spring 2022 for a total of 12 interviews. The purpose of the interviews was to gather information about implementation of teaching and departmental review processes in place at other independent schools. We provided a $50 Amazon gift card to each participant upon completion of the interview.

We first interviewed one staff member from each of four independent school service organizations in fall 2021: the National Association of Independent Schools, Folio, Mastery Collaborative, and 1SchoolHouse. These four organizations provide services (e.g., technology platforms, professional development) and resources (e.g., examples of observation tools or teacher/student competencies) to help independent schools design and implement processes for reviewing teaching practice. These four interviewees work with a diverse group of independent schools across the United States. and were able to give us a broad overview of common practices and the state of the field among the schools they serve.

In spring 2022, we interviewed administrators at eight independent schools: Washington International School, Waynflete, Vermont Academy, Pomfret School, Holton-Arms School, Oxford Academy, The Dalton School, and Mercersburg Academy. We contacted an additional eight independent schools that did not respond to our invitation. We spoke with school administrators who were responsible for designing and implementing teaching and departmental review processes, such as Deans of Academics, Deans of Faculty, Deans of Curriculum and Instruction, and Deans of Professional Growth. We obtained these schools' names through snowball sampling, asking each interviewee for suggestions of independent schools reputed to have high-quality teaching or departmental reviews, or who had revised their systems.

Interview Protocol Design and Data Collection

We used semistructured interview protocols—one for Andover chairs and another for the independent school service organizations—which we developed after reviewing documentation describing the teaching and departmental review processes. We shared the Andover chair protocol with Andover leadership for their input (but not the independent school service organization protocol), but the research team retained final editorial control of the question wording. Two qualitative researchers led the interviews.

The semistructured protocol allowed for balance and consistency in the questions asked and ensured coverage of important content while allowing respondents to elaborate or offer unsolicited input. The protocols covered a range of topics related to teaching and departmental review processes and respondents' perceptions of these processes. For example, we asked questions about the use of surveys to gather student feedback, timing and frequency of teaching review processes, the use of informal and formal reviews, instructional coaching, peer observations, and departmental reviews/self-study processes. We also asked a set of broader questions about implementation challenges and enablers.

The interviews with Andover department chairs and independent school staff framed the questions to elicit information about that school's current processes while the interviews with service organizations framed the questions around common practices and policies among each organization's member schools. In addition, we asked the interviewee at each service organization to suggest several independent schools that were in the process of updating their teaching review processes we should contact.

Interview Data Analysis

We used an iterative approach to coding and followed established qualitative research procedures for ensuring reliability (Denzin and Lincoln, 2003; Lincoln and Guba, 1985; Miles and Huberman, 1994; Strauss and Corbin, 1993). To support the analysis process, we developed a broad initial coding scheme that was guided by the interview protocol. Codes included, for example, familiarity/experience with each component of the annual and periodic teaching review processes, perceptions of the teaching review process as helpful for development or a compliance exercise, and descriptions of departmental review activities.

These codes allowed us to categorize the data by topic (e.g., to review all the excerpts about the annual informal review process together) and analyze them to pull out themes. The RAND co-leads developed the initial coding scheme and coded the interviews by logging faculty members' responses to each interview question in a spreadsheet. Throughout the data-collection process, the two co-leads reviewed interview responses to surface additional codes that reflected emergent themes. Through these discussions, the team resolved ambiguities and made decisions to add new codes and themes. We revised the coding scheme and documented decision rules as necessary. As we conducted interviews and coded excerpts in a spreadsheet, we logged a running set of emergent themes and met to debrief on the patterns that we observed. These emergent themes then formed the basis for our systematic analysis of coded excerpts.

Once all interviews were conducted and coding was complete, we conducted a systematic review of coded excerpts to verify the emergent themes that we identified and determine whether there were any additional themes. We drew on established techniques to identify themes (Bernard, Wutich, and Ryan, 2016; Ryan and Bernard, 2003), including looking for repetition, similarities, and differences between sets of data (e.g., similar responses across current chairs, or chairs who identified as people of color). The co–principal investigators reviewed all the excerpts relevant to each code and developed inductive second-level codes, where appropriate, to analyze themes under each code. These second-level codes focused on what the excerpt described (e.g., the specific components of the formal teaching review process), what was happening (e.g., whether the chair implemented that aspect of the review process regularly), and why (e.g., challenges that prevented the chair from implementing that component of the formal review). Although we did keep track of the number of respondents who spoke to a particular second-level code for the purpose of understanding the prevalence of various themes or topics within our sample and within teacher subgroups, we did not use the data to create quantitative indicators.

We took multiple steps to ensure the integrity of our findings, such as searching for and examining both confirming and disconfirming evidence (Denzin, 2006). In addition, we leveraged multiple approaches to identify themes, including keeping a running record of potential themes throughout the data-collection process, and conducting systematic analysis of coded excerpts.

Interview Limitations

The purpose of conducting the interviews with independent school administrators was to broadly understand how some other independent schools conduct teaching and departmental review processes and how they are approaching revising these processes. The purpose of the interviews with Andover department chairs was to understand how the faculty largely responsible for implementing teaching and departmental reviews conduct that work in practice, and their perceptions of how well (or poorly) those processes operate. Responses from these interviews were intended to complement the literature review and ExpertLens data.

These interview data do have several limitations. First, we only interviewed a small convenience sample of independent school administrators. Although we strove to select institutions that could be considered peers of Andover, we certainly did not capture the full range of possible approaches to teaching and departmental review at independent schools. However, this was not the intent, and we did reach some saturation in responses among our interviewees. Second, although we interviewed a current and former department chair in every academic department at Andover, their views about the teaching and departmental review processes may not represent those of the faculty at large. However, the department chair interviews were not intended to be representative of all Andover faculty. Third, interview responses are, by definition, subject to self-report bias. Thus, our investigation was limited to teachers' perceptions of the teaching and departmental review processes and we were not able to independently verify their responses.

ExpertLens

Overview of ExpertLens

ExpertLens is an online platform for conducting stakeholder engagement and expert elicitation activities using a Delphi method (Dalal et al., 2011). It has been used in over 30 research studies funded by government agencies, foundations, and private companies to engage professionals such as clinicians and government officials, as well as lay people such as patients and caregivers (Jilani et al., 2022; Khodyakov et al., 2019; Kim et al., 2018).

ExpertLens is based on key principles of the modified-Delphi method, which allows participants to independently answer questions, see how their answers compare with those of other participants, and discuss them before providing their final response to questions, which can be modified after the initial results have been discussed (Fitch et al., 2001). ExpertLens, however, replaces the in-person discussion in the modified-Delphi method with online interaction among participants that takes place using asynchronous and completely anonymous discussion boards moderated by an experienced moderator using a standard set of discussion facilitation techniques (Khodyakov et al., 2020).

The Delphi-based methodology used by ExpertLens is particularly useful in studies on controversial topics and is designed to help a diverse group of stakeholders generate and prioritize solutions to complex problems such as teaching reviews (Beiderbeck et al., 2021). Teaching reviews involve balancing the use of standardized or at least comparable tools and policies to evaluate teaching practices, which are inherently varied, individualized, and nuanced. Although RAND researchers have not used ExpertLens in education studies before this one, the Delphi method itself is a widely used method in education research (Robertson et al., 2000; Clayton, 1997).

The main goal of the ExpertLens process was to learn faculty's views about a series of potential revisions to Andover's teaching evaluation policy and department self-review. To achieve this goal, we conducted two three-round ExpertLens panels described below.

How ExpertLens worked at Andover

We obtained a list of all 158 teaching faculty from Andover who are subject to the faculty rating system described in Chapter 4, and we invited all 158 to participate in each of three rounds of ExpertLens.

We divided the 158 faculty into two panels of 79 people each—Panel A and Panel B. We divided the 158 faculty into two panels because our experience shows that having larger groups makes the online discussion round onerous with too many comments for a participant to read or react to, and smaller panels may not generate enough useful information because of the voluntary nature of participation and attrition common in Delphi panels (Khodyakov et al., 2011).

To ensure that both Panel A and B were similar in faculty composition, we balanced them on faculty gender, years of teaching experience at Andover, race, and STEM versus non-STEM teaching. Panel A members only saw the anonymous ratings and comments from Panel A, and the same applied for Panel B. We posed identically worded recommendations and questions to Panel A and B at all three rounds of ExpertLens, so we combine their ratings throughout this report.

Each panel completed the following three ExpertLens rounds.

Round 1

Andover staff reviewed a list of 14 faculty evaluation and feedback practices that we developed and rated them on two 9-point Likert scales: *helpfulness* (the extent to which each evaluation practice could help with teacher development) and *feasibility* (the extent to which each evaluation practice could be reasonable for Andover to execute). For each practice, we briefly explained what each practice entails and how it might work in implementation. In addition to providing numeric responses, participants were asked to explain their ratings using open-text boxes (see Figure A.1). Of the 158 invited faculty members across the two panels, 100 (55 percent) answered at least one question.

FIGURE A.1
How a Potential Recommendation Appeared in Round 1 of ExpertLens

Potential recommendation 1: Andover should develop a written document that lists the academic, social, and emotional competencies that PA graduates should possess.

Overview: Andover should articulate the collective set of competencies to which all elements of the academic, extracurricular, and residential-life programs contribute. Working from the school-wide list of desired student competencies, departments and individual courses would identify which student competencies they develop. The end goal is for the collection of diploma-required courses to build over a series of four years the desired set of competencies.

How it might work: A widely representative Andover committee would develop the school-wide list of desired student competencies for an Andover graduate over the course of a year, soliciting faculty feedback. In the year following the publication of the list of Andover-wide desired student competencies, each department would work together to determine which subset their courses can or should develop over the sequence of its diploma-required courses. Individual faculty would identify in both their syllabi and the course listing in the Course of Study the specific competencies that the course develops. Every six years, Andover would revisit these school-wide competencies to modify or update them if needed. (RAND proposes six-year cycles so updates occur once during each six-year department chair appointment.)

How helpful would this recommendation be for your development as a teacher?

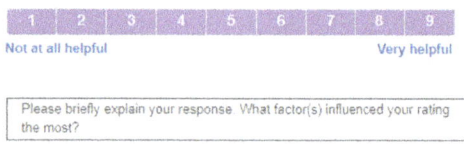

Please briefly explain your response. What factor(s) influenced your rating the most?

How feasible would this recommendation be for Andover to execute?

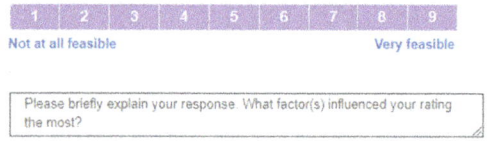

Please briefly explain your response. What factor(s) influenced your rating the most?

Round 2

In this round, participants saw how their own responses compared with those of other participants and whether there was consensus among them. Round 1 results were presented on a chart that showed the distribution of the group's responses, along with the median and interquartile range. A color-coded statement stating whether the group reached agreement and what they thought about helpfulness and feasibility of each evaluation practice was shown above each chart (see Figure A.2). Participants could also see how their own responses compared to those of teachers of color, female teachers, and those with ten or more years of experience. In addition to summarizing rating results, we also analyzed Round One comments that explained participants' ratings and presented comment summaries next to each chart (see below). Of the 158 invited participants, 76 (48 percent) reviewed round 1 results by logging into ExpertLens at least once during round 2.

FIGURE A.2
How the Results for a Potential Recommendation Appeared in Round 2 of ExpertLens

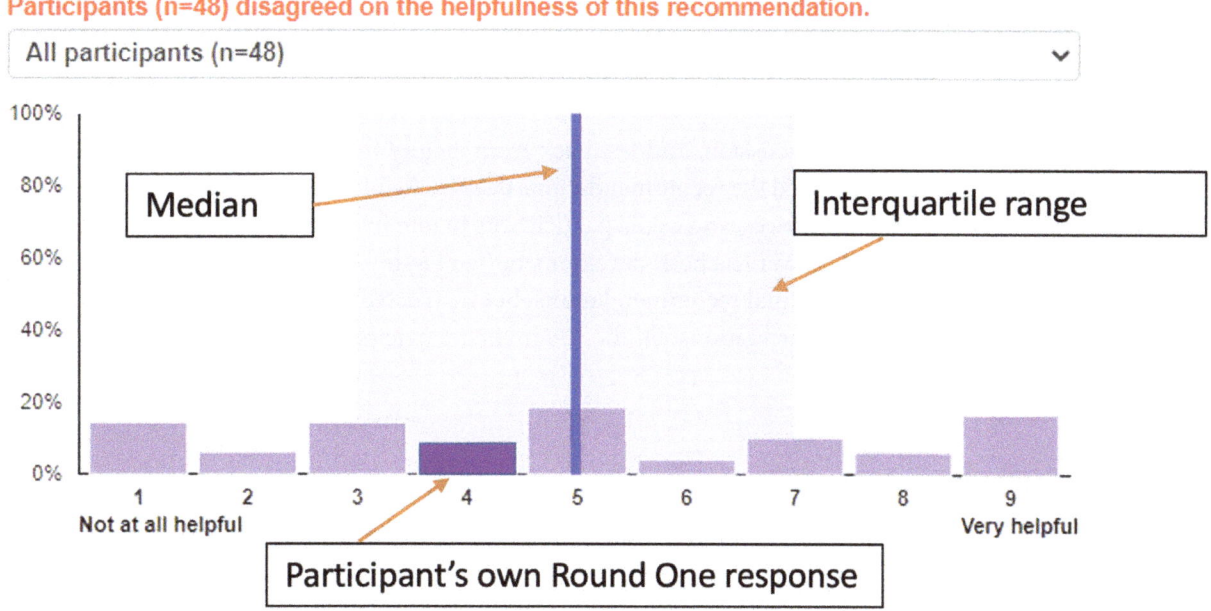

Faculty members also discussed round 1 results using asynchronous virtual discussion boards moderated by one of the project leads. Participants' comments were completely anonymous. They could either start a new discussion thread or respond to a comment posted by the moderator or another participant (see Figure A.3). Of the 76 participants who reviewed round 1 results, 34 (45 percent) participated in the discussion by posting 237 comments (on average, seven comments per participant).

FIGURE A.3
How the Anonymous Discussion Board Appeared in Round 2 of ExpertLens

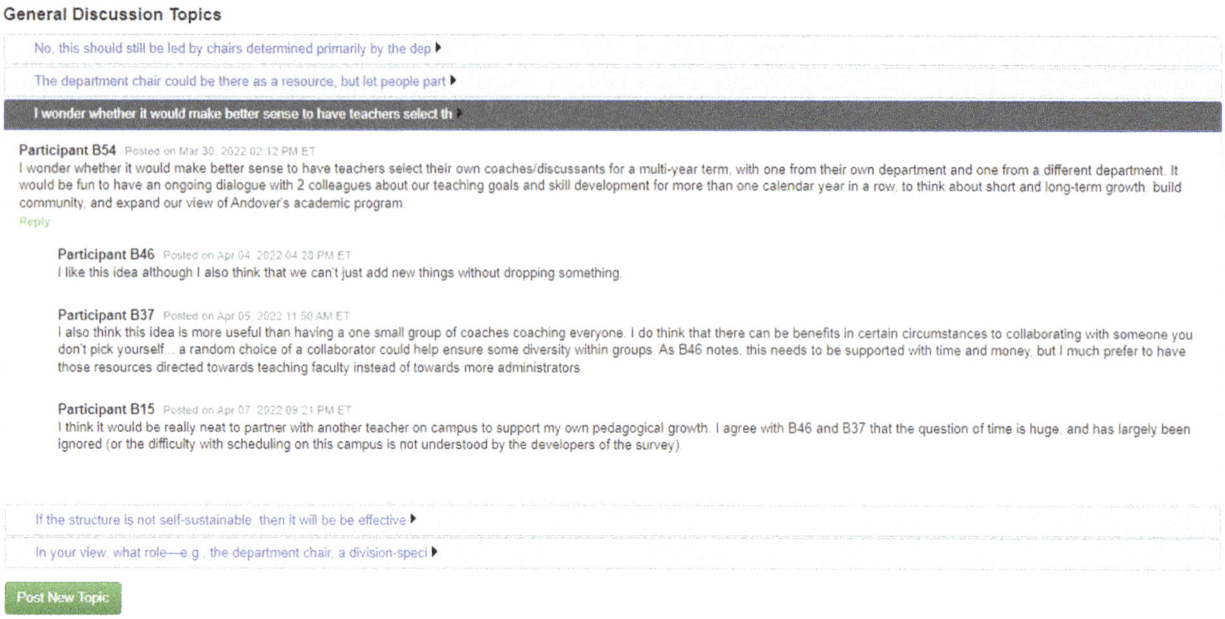

Round 3

Based on round 1 results, round 2 discussion, and feedback from faculty that participation took more time than they would have liked, we dropped the recommendations deemed helpful in round 1, modified and condensed the remaining evaluation practices, and asked participants to rate five revised recommendations only in terms of their helpfulness for Andover teachers' development (see Figure A.4). For transparency purposes, we presented the results for all 14 original recommendations, but instructed participants not to re-rate them and only rate the five revised recommendations. Of the 158 invited participants, 61 (39 percent) answered at least one question in round 3.

FIGURE A.4
How a Revised Recommendation Appeared in Round 3 of ExpertLens

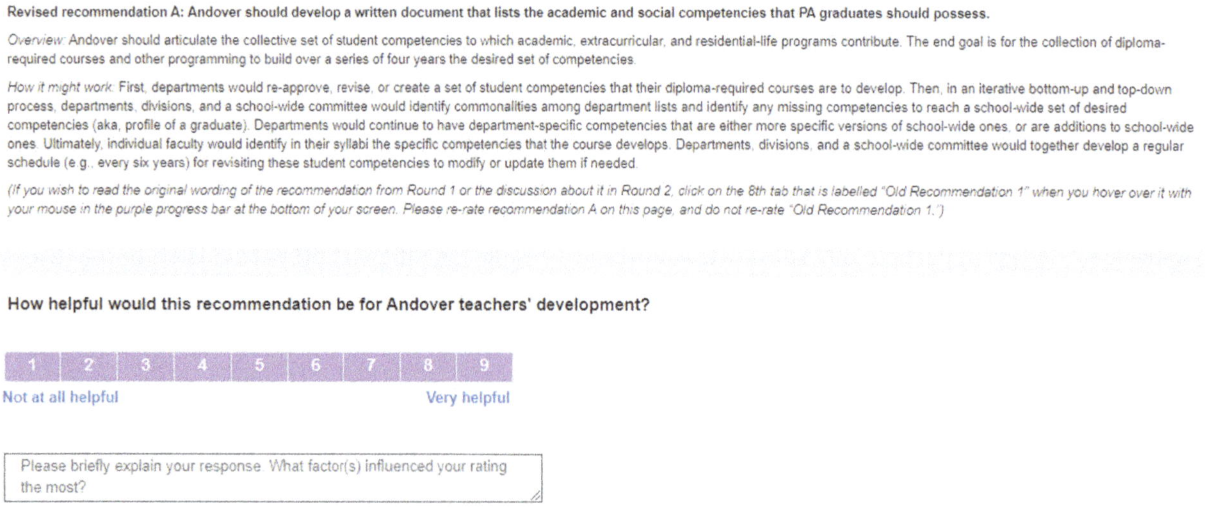

How We Determined Panel Decisions in ExpertLens

ExpertLens automatically determined the panel's decision after rounds 1 and 3 by relying on a multistep algorithm commonly used in modified-Delphi panels that use 9-point Likert-type rating scales (Fitch et al., 2001). Figure A.5 depicts this algorithm: The first three steps are designed to look at the distribution of panelists' responses to determine whether they agree or disagree with each other, whereas the fourth step uses the panel's median response to determine the panel's decision. These decisions are color-coded in the display within ExpertLens to help participants quickly glance at the numeric results and determine whether the panel's decision is positive (green font), uncertain (blue font), or negative (red font).

FIGURE A.5
Algorithm to Calculate Panel Decisions in ExpertLens

Step 1: Calculate Interpercentile Range (IPR)
- IPR = 70th percentile – 30th percentiles

Step 2: Calculate IPR Adjusted for Symmetry (IPRAS)
- IPRAS = 2.35 + (AI × 1.5)
  AI is Asymmetry Index, or the distance between the central point of the IPR and 5 (the central point of the 1–9 rating scale)

Step 3: Determine the Existence of Disagreement
- If IPR > IPRAS, there is disagreement.
- If IPR < IPRAS, there is no disagreement.

Step 4: Determine Panel Decision
- Disagreement automatically produces uncertain panel decision.
- If there is no disagreement, then the median determines panel decision:
  - If a median score is between 6.5 and 9, then the strategy is helpful or feasible
  - If a median score is between 3.5 and 6, then the strategy is of uncertain helpfulness or feasibility
  - If a median score is between 1 and 3, then the strategy is not helpful or feasible

Round 1 and 3 Results

Table A.2 provides both the full wording of the 14 recommendations, as well as the median rating among faculty and 25th percentile and 75th percentile rating of, first the helpfulness of the recommendation for teaching, and, second, the feasibility of the recommendation.

TABLE A.2
Faculty Ratings of Helpfulness and Feasibility of 14 Potential Recommendations in Round 1

Potential Recommendation	Number of Faculty Who Rated It	Median Rating	25th Percentile Rating	75th Percentile Rating	Faculty Overall Decision
1: Andover should develop a written document that lists the academic, social, and emotional competencies that Phillips Academy Andover graduates should possess. *Overview:* Andover should articulate the collective set of competencies to which all elements of the academic, extracurricular, and residential-life programs contribute. Working from the school-wide list of desired student competencies, departments and individual courses would identify which student competencies they develop. The end goal is for the collection of diploma-required courses to build over a series of four years the desired set of competencies. *How it might work:* A widely representative Andover committee would develop the school-wide list of desired student competencies over the course of a year, soliciting faculty feedback. In the year following the publication of the list of Andover-wide desired student competencies, each department would work together to determine which subset their courses can or should develop over the sequence of its diploma-required courses. Individual faculty would identify in both their syllabi and the course listing in the *Course of Study* the specific competencies that the course develops. Every six years, Andover would revisit these school-wide competencies to modify or update them if needed. (RAND proposes six-year cycles so updates occur once during each six-year department chair appointment.)	H: 98 F: 94	H: 5.5 F: 5	H: 3 F: 3	H: 7 F: 7	H: Uncertain F: Uncertain
2: Andover should restructure and rename the Evaluation Committee to consist of teaching faculty trained as instructional coaches who would lead the teacher development process. *Overview:* In its expanded role, the renamed Evaluation Committee would be the central group responsible for coordinating, documenting, and periodically updating Andover's teacher professional development system. The professional development system would be focused on teaching faculty's professional growth, with a separate system not run by this committee for ensuring that Andover courses meet minimum expectations (described in recommendation 10). *How it might work:* Andover teaching faculty would run for election to serve as one of approximately five total instructional coaches on the committee. Instructional coaches would serve for 3-5 years. Committee members would obtain substantial course relief to gain the necessary amount of time and schedule flexibility to perform their expanded duties. (See recommendation 3, 7, and 8 about expanded duties.) Committee members would obtain at least one full week of training each year on instructional coaching, how to give actionable feedback, anti-bias training, and training on observation inter-rater reliability among the instructional coaches. The committee would be diverse across disciplines.	H: 95 F: 90	H: 5 F: 5	H: 3 F: 3	H: 8 F: 6	H: Uncertain F: Uncertain

Table A.2—continued

Potential Recommendation	Number of Faculty Who Rated It	Median Rating	25th Percentile Rating	75th Percentile Rating	Faculty Overall Decision
3: Each teaching faculty member should meet with their assigned instructional coach from the Evaluation Committee twice each year to discuss their goals for that year. *Overview:* Each teaching faculty member would meet with their assigned instructional coach, rather than the department chair, in the fall and spring each year. The purpose of these meetings is for each teacher to have one-on-one time to talk about their teaching with a trained instructional coach, to set a professional goal for the year, and to reflect on their pursuit of that goal in the spring. This annual goal-setting conversation would be developmental—i.e., not for the purpose of evaluating teachers' performance—and would not occur during the years that the faculty member participates in the periodic teaching review process described in recommendation 4. *How it might work:* Each instructional coach on the renamed evaluation committee would have a "caseload" of approximately 30 teachers for these annual conversations. The instructional coaches on the committee would develop a conversation guide for these fall and spring conversations. The coaches would also become a central resource who are informed about the various sources of funding for professional development at Andover. With the aid of an administrative assistant for the instructional coaching committee, the committee would be responsible for uploading notes or documents from these conversations into a central, electronic database that teachers can also access.	H: 94 F: 91	H: 5 F: 5	H: 3 F: 2	H: 7 F: 6.5	H: Uncertain F: Uncertain
4: Every few years, each teaching faculty should receive a more comprehensive teaching review. *Overview:* In lieu of the annual goal-setting conversations described in recommendation 3, each teaching faculty would receive a comprehensive review of their classroom teaching every few years (see recommendation 5 about the frequency). For brevity, we refer to this as a "periodic teaching review" from here on. This review would retain most of the elements of Andover's current teaching evaluation system, with some changes as detailed in the next paragraph. *How it might work:* The periodic teaching review would still include two classroom observations by the evaluation committee member (i.e., instructional coach); one classroom observation by the department chair; the pre- and post-observation conversations; the residential, athletic, and advisory components (until such time as Andover updates those elements); and the culminating conversation with the Dean of Faculty and Dean of Studies. The following are RAND's proposed changes: (1) the peer observation would shift out of teaching reviews to departmental self-studies (recommendation 13); (2) the instructional coach committee would revise several forms for the review process (recommendation 7); (3) teachers would write their reflection piece at the end of the periodic teaching review process (recommendation 9); and (4) an instructional coach would oversee the periodic teaching review (recommendation 8).	H: 89 F: 85	H: 6 F: 6	H: 4 F: 4	H: 7 F: 7	H: Uncertain F: Uncertain
5: The periodic teaching review should occur every *three* years, starting in a teacher's third year at Andover. *Overview:* RAND recommends that the periodic teaching review occur every three years for all faculty starting in their third year. This would replace Andover's existing policy to review faculty in their third year, eighth year, and then every eight years thereafter. *How it might work:* During a teacher's third, sixth, ninth, twelfth, etc., year of teaching at Andover, the teacher would receive the periodic teaching review described in recommendation 4. In all other years, the teacher would have a fall and a spring goal-setting conversation with an instructional coach as described in recommendation 3.	H: 90 F: 89	H: 5 F: 4	H: 3 F: 2	H: 7 F: 6	H: Uncertain F: Uncertain

Table A.2—continued

Potential Recommendation	Number of Faculty Who Rated It	Median Rating	25th Percentile Rating	75th Percentile Rating	Faculty Overall Decision
6: Andover should identify a written list of desired teacher competencies designed to elicit and develop the desired student competencies. *Overview:* Andover would identify a collective set of competencies which teachers should exemplify in their classrooms, including diversity, equity and inclusion. The teacher competencies would leave room for teacher autonomy and focus on a core set of widely-shared teaching practices. The teacher competencies would be designed to elicit and develop the desired student competencies and would align with Andover's core values. Here's an example of a teacher competency: "Units are designed around essential questions and inquiry-driven, active learning informs activities and assessments." *How it might work:* After the student competencies are developed (see recommendation 1), the Academic Council and instructional coaches could jointly develop these teacher competencies over the course of a school year. The competencies could build off of Andover's previous, related work such as the "Andover Design/Build Standards and Teacher Competencies" and examples from other public and independent schools, which RAND can provide.	H: 90 F: 87	H: 6 F: 5	H: 3 F: 3	H: 8 F: 7	H: Uncertain F: Disagreement
7: The instructional coach committee should integrate Andover's student and teacher competencies into the annual and periodic teaching review process. *Overview:* The annual goal-setting conversations each faculty member has with their instructional coach and the periodic teaching review that occurs every three years should be structured to ensure that faculty members are helping students develop the school-wide competencies and exemplifying the desired teacher competencies. *How it might work:* The instructional coaches will revise the existing classroom observation tool to prompt for observed competency development. The observation tool should include concrete examples of specific student and teacher actions that indicate that the desired school-wide student competencies are being developed. The instructional coaches will also develop pre- and post-observation conversation guides to prompt for discussion of student competency development, desired teacher competencies, and to include the course syllabus.	H: 90 F: 86	H: 5 F: 5	H: 2 F: 2	H: 7 F: 7	H: Disagreement F: Uncertain
8: The instructional coaches should oversee the periodic teaching review. *Overview:* The instructional coach, rather than the department chair, would coordinate the periodic teaching review. *How it might work:* Each instructional coach will have a caseload of approximately ten faculty who are scheduled to undergo the periodic teaching review that year. The instructional coach would lead the fall meeting with the reviewee to set their goals and explain the process for the review that year. The instructional coach would also lead the spring summative meeting, which the department chair, Dean of Faculty, and Dean of Studies would also attend.	H: 89 F: 86	H: 4 F: 5	H: 2 F: 2	H: 7 F: 7	H: Uncertain F: Uncertain
9: Faculty participating in the periodic teaching review should write a brief self-reflection at the end of the review rather than the beginning. *Overview:* Faculty members who are undergoing the periodic teaching review (as described in recommendation 4) should write a brief self-reflection at the end of the year in which they are reviewed instead of the beginning of the year, as is current policy. *How it might work:* Faculty members would write this brief self-reflection after the spring summative meeting. The instructional coach committee would design a template for this self-reflection that would include maximum page length (e.g., 2 pages) and a few (e.g., 2–4) topics or question prompts that would encourage the teacher to think ahead to the next year, including about student competencies and the teaching competencies. This self-reflection would serve as a starting point for the next fall's goal-setting conversation between faculty member and coach.	H: 87 F: 83	H: 7 F: 8	H: 5 F: 5	H: 8 F: 9	H: Helpful F: Feasible

Table A.2—continued

Potential Recommendation	Number of Faculty Who Rated It	Median Rating	25th Percentile Rating	75th Percentile Rating	Faculty Overall Decision
10: Andover should repurpose the school-wide anonymous student survey to ensure Andover courses meet and exceed a minimum set of expectations. *Overview:* The scope of the existing anonymous student survey would be narrowed to be one data source, but likely not the main one. Andover administrators would use the survey to identify any concerns about faculty members' performances. This survey would not be intended to help teachers to refine their courses or inform instructional decisionmaking. Instead, questions for course refinement would appear in a separate student survey that individual departments design on their own (see recommendation 11). *How it might work:* The anonymous student survey would be shortened to take fewer than 10 minutes to complete and would run in each trimester of the year in each class the teacher instructs. The survey would solely consist of school-wide low-inference questions like teachers showing up on time for class, prompt grading, and the teacher being prepared for class. A copy of the survey questions would be shared so all faculty know what questions students answer about each course. Using prior research about strategies to reduce racial and gender bias in students' responses, RAND can provide a sample script to Andover for teachers to use and lightly adapt to read ahead of time to students. Andover could produce an end-of-year report for each teacher that presents an average of the midpoint (i.e., median) ratings on each survey item from each survey administration, as well as the range of scores on each survey item. This approach will minimize the impact of outlier scores. The department chair will review these end-of-year reports and discuss any noteworthy result first with the relevant faculty member and then with additional administrators as the conditions warrant.	H: 88 F: 85	H: 5 F: 6	H: 1 F: 4	H: 7 F: 8	H: Uncertain F: Uncertain
11: Separate from and in addition to the anonymous school-wide student survey, faculty should be encouraged to run their own student surveys to inform their instructional decisionmaking. *Overview:* Each year, department chairs, together with their faculty, should decide whether to design and administer a department-wide student survey, or else encourage individual faculty run their own student surveys. These surveys would not be used for accountability purposes and results would not automatically be shared outside the department. Ideally, teachers would use the results to make refinements their courses and adjust their instruction. *How it might work:* These surveys could be administered in whatever software the department or faculty prefers (e.g., Canvas, Google Forms, Microsoft Forms, etc.) and at whatever time point(s) during the year is preferred. The surveys need not be anonymous, and items could be closed- or open-ended on whatever topics are of interest to the department or faculty person that year.	H: 87 F: 85	H: 9 F: 9	H: 7 F: 7	H: 9 F: 9	H: Helpful F: Feasible
12: Each year, each department should select at least one instructional self-study topic for the year. *Overview:* To encourage a culture of continuous growth and inquiry, department chairs should lead faculty to select at least one instructional self-study topic each year, with some topics recurring every six years. This department-wide instructional focus should be the department chair's main substantive focus. *How it might work:* Each department chair would share the proposed topic each fall with the Dean of Studies for the Dean's approval to ensure certain topics are covered on schedule. each spring, the department would submit a short, written document (ideally, a copy of a policy that the department has adopted) to the Dean of Studies. Self-study topics might be wide-ranging and could include pedagogy, staff development and mentoring, curriculum or assessment. But every six years (a frequency RAND selected to align with a chair's six-year tenure), the department would revisit each of the following subjects: (1) grade norming to ensure faculty grade student work in similar ways; (2) curriculum mapping for vertically and horizontally aligned courses so that (a) multiple sections of a class cover similar content, and (b) students are prepared to progress from one level of course to the next throughout the department's course sequence; and (3) developing a short plan about how the department may evolve over the next five years.	H: 85 F: 84	H: 7 F: 7	H: 5 F: 5	H: 9 F: 8	H: Helpful F: Feasible

Table A.2—continued

Potential Recommendation	Number of Faculty Who Rated It	Median Rating	25th Percentile Rating	75th Percentile Rating	Faculty Overall Decision
13: To inform departmental self-studies, each faculty member should observe at least one class of another faculty member within their department each year.	H: 86 F: 86	H: 9 F: 9	H: 7 F: 7	H: 9 F: 9	H: Helpful F: Feasible
Process: To encourage ongoing departmental conversations about instruction and to help build a coherent culture within a department, faculty members would observe at least one class of at least one fellow faculty member within their department (or in a small department, within their division) each year. *How it might work:* The observations would not be evaluative, and they would not necessarily follow a written classroom observation tool. The observations could focus on the departmental self-study topic for that year (e.g., teacher question asking) and/or on topics that the observed teacher wishes. Peer observations would not be included in the periodic teacher evaluation process.					
14: Andover should invite external observers to visit on a periodic basis to support departments' self-study process.	H: 86 F: 86	H: 6 F: 5	H: 3 F: 3	H: 8 F: 7.5	H: Uncertain F: Uncertain
Process: To provide departments with new ideas from peer institutions and an independent review, Andover would enlist teachers from other schools or other education professionals to perform departmental reviews. *How it might work:* Once every six years (i.e., once during each chair's tenure), teachers from other peer high schools or educators from public, private, and small colleges would visit Andover to observe a set of classes in a given department, interview the department chair, some department faculty, and administrators as relevant, and review the departments' standards, policies, and course offerings. The external teachers would provide a written summary of recommendations to the department chair and the Dean of Studies. This process would be separate from and in addition to Andover's accreditation process.					

NOTE: All 158 faculty were invited to rate the 14 recommendations on a range of 1 to 9, where 1 was "not at all helpful" or "not at all feasible" and 9 was "very helpful" or "very feasible". H = faculty rating of "How helpful would this recommendation be for your development as a teacher?" F = faculty rating of "How feasible do you think this recommendation would be for Andover to execute?" Faculty overall decision was one of four potential determinations—helpful/feasible; uncertain helpfulness/feasibility; unhelpful/not feasible; or disagreement—and was calculated automatically by the ExpertLens algorithm.

TABLE A.3
Faculty Ratings of Helpfulness of Potential Recommendations in Round 3

Potential Recommendation	Number of Faculty Who Rated It	Median Rating	25th Percentile Rating	75th Percentile Rating	Faculty Overall Determination
Revised recommendation A: Andover should develop a written document that lists the academic and social competencies that Phillips Academy Andover graduates should possess. *Overview*: Andover should articulate the collective set of student competencies to which academic, extracurricular, and residential-life programs contribute. The end goal is for the collection of diploma-required courses and other programming to build over a series of four years the desired set of competencies. *How it might work*: First, departments would re-approve, revise, or create a set of student competencies that their diploma-required courses are to develop. Then, in an iterative bottom-up and top-down process, departments, divisions, and a school-wide committee would identify commonalities among department lists and identify any missing competencies to reach a school-wide set of desired competencies (aka, profile of a graduate). Departments would continue to have department-specific competencies that are either more specific versions of school-wide ones, or are additions to school-wide ones. Ultimately, individual faculty would identify in their syllabi the specific competencies that the course develops. Departments, divisions, and a school-wide committee would together develop a regular schedule (e.g., every six years) for revisiting these student competencies to modify or update them if needed.	60	7	3	7	Helpful
Revised recommendation B: Andover should identify a written list of desired teaching competencies designed to develop the desired student competencies. *Overview*: Andover would identify a collective set of competencies which teachers should exemplify in their classrooms, including promoting diversity, equity, and inclusion. The teaching competencies would leave room for teacher autonomy and focus on a core set of widely shared teaching practices. The teaching competencies would be designed to elicit and develop the desired student competencies and would align with Andover's core values. *How it might work*: After the student competencies are developed (see recommendation A), departments could then develop a list of desired teaching competencies. Then, in a similar iterative bottom-up and top-down process, departments, divisions, and a school-wide committee would identify commonalities among department lists and identify any missing competencies to reach a short list of school-wide set of desired teaching competencies that are potentially complemented by a set of department-specific, more detailed expressions of those skills. The school-wide competencies will be general, and the departments can then develop department-specific competencies. Departments, divisions, and a school-wide committee would review the teaching competencies on a regular schedule (e.g., every six years) to modify or update them if needed.	57	6	2	7	Uncertain

Table A.3—continued

Potential Recommendation	Number of Faculty Who Rated It	Median Rating	25th Percentile Rating	75th Percentile Rating	Faculty Overall Determination
Revised recommendation C: Each year, a department chair (or assistant chair where relevant) should hold one 30-minute developmental conversation with each faculty member and observe their class at least once.	56	7	5.75	9	Helpful
Overview: In round 1 and 2 feedback, most faculty preferred that their department chair, rather than an instructional coach from a school-wide committee, lead the teacher development process. Most faculty also felt that two annual conversations was impractical due to lack of time. Therefore RAND recommends that (1) either a department chair or assistant chair have one developmental conversation each year with each faculty person; (2) these annual conversations with faculty would reference the department-specific lens on teaching competencies; (3) Andover identify ways to free up time for chairs or assistant chairs to enact these annual conversations, including hiring a full-time project manager at Andover tasked with running the logistics for the annual conversations and the formal teaching review described in the next recommendation, and (4) Andover provide all chairs and assistant chairs with training at the outset of their term and also written guidance outlining a common process for these developmental conversations and how to support the development of teaching practices.					
Revised recommendation D: As is current practice, a department chair should oversee the formal teaching review. The formal teaching review would retain most of the same elements and would still occur on a staggered, but slightly more frequent schedule.	55	7	5	8	Helpful
Overview: Because of faculty preference in rounds 1 and 2 for department-led teaching reviews as opposed to a process run by a substantially better-resourced Evaluation Committee (renamed Instructional Coaching Committee), RAND now proposes that Andover invest more resources in the form of training, written guidance, and administrative staff to support department chairs to lead the formal teaching review process. In this revised recommendation, department chairs would oversee the periodic formal teaching review. Andover would retain the general structure of its current formal evaluation process as laid out in the *Faculty Handbook*, with some exceptions we describe next.					
How it might work: The schedule for the formal reviews would be similar to current practice in that formal reviews would first start in a teacher's third year, then in their sixth year, and then every *five or six* years thereafter instead of every eight years. With three exceptions, the elements of the formal review would remain the same. The two proposed changes to the process are to: (1) eliminate the Evaluation Committee's classroom observations since committee members lack sufficient course relief to allow for the match of observers by department or division to reviewed faculty, and (2) remove the peer observation from the formal review and instead make peer observations a part of departmental self-study process.					

Table A.3—continued

Potential Recommendation	Number of Faculty Who Rated It	Median Rating	25th Percentile Rating	75th Percentile Rating	Faculty Overall Determination
Revised recommendation E: Departments and/or faculty should field their own surveys each year of students to make instructional decisions. Separately, Andover should substantially revise the school-wide anonymous student survey and use it to ensure Andover courses meet and exceed a minimum set of expectations. *Overview*: Each year, faculty and/or their departments should run their own student surveys (anonymous or not) to help inform their own instructional decisionmaking, as is currently done by many faculty at Andover. Separate from those faculty-run surveys, Andover should significantly revise the anonymous student survey to serve the administration's need to ensure "course basics" are met. *How it might work*: RAND recommends that Andover substantially change the current student survey administered in Qualtrics as follows: 1. Cut the anonymous Qualtrics survey down to 5 minutes or less. 2. Run the survey for every course in each trimester, and run it prior to midterms. 3. Ask students via a message from the administration to fill out a survey for each course the student takes that trimester. Students can fill these out during an advising period. 4. Add a script addressed to students at the beginning of the survey that draws on prior research to reduce bias in student responses. 5. Restrict the questions to topics related to professionalism such as a teacher being on time to class, whether the student received a written syllabus and a written grading policy by the first class of the semester, and whether the teacher posts all assignments no later than the end of the class period. There would be no questions about higher-order concepts like quality of instruction or fairness of grading. 6. The Andover administration would disseminate an automatically generated report after each survey administration to the relevant faculty person and that faculty person's department chair to surface issues and to give teachers the chance to address any issues that arise.	53	7	4	8	Helpful

Analysis of Comments Faculty Provided in ExpertLens

While ExpertLens automatically applies this algorithm to round 1 and round 3 rating data, we analyzed qualitative data manually. Participants provided two types of qualitative data: explanations of their ratings and discussion comments.

To better explain experts' perspectives, we thematically analyzed their explanations of ratings provided using a previously developed approach (Khodyakov et al., 2019; Khodyakov et al., 2017). We grouped all Round One comments based on their numeric response (ratings 1–3, 4–6, and 7–9, which correspond to low, medium, and high levels of helpfulness and feasibility). Doing so is consistent with the mixed-methods nature of the ExpertLens methodology. Three researchers experienced with coding ExpertLens data coded all round 1 explanations inductively to identify common emergent themes in Excel. Coders coded the data for the same evaluation practices in both panels to ensure coding consistency. One project lead reviewed all coding results to ensure consistency between coders and panels; another project lead reviewed the results with a goal of ensuring correct interpretation of comments. The team discussed any coding inconsistencies or discrepancies until consensus was reached. Results of this comment coding were presented to participants in a tabular format, served as the basis for creating round 2 discussion comments posted by the discussion moderator, and informed the revision of evaluation practices shown to participants in round 3.

The two RAND project leads used the comments from Rounds 1 and 2 to inform its revisions of potential recommendations in round 3.

APPENDIX B

Andover's Statement of Purpose, Values, and Academic Vision

This appendix provides the school's statement of purpose, values, and academic vision. These can be found at www.andover.edu/about.

Andover's Statement of Purpose

Phillips Academy's Constitution charges the faculty to teach "youth from every quarter" to aspire equally to knowledge and goodness. This obligation challenges students to develop what is finest in themselves and others, for others and themselves. Phillips Academy is committed to nurturing an intentionally diverse, inclusive community that encourages students and adults to respect, inspire, and learn from one another. Guided by the ideal of non sibi, leading lives "not for self," the Phillips Academy community promotes a balance of intellectual curiosity, engagement, leadership, and service in the pursuit of excellence: academic, civic, and moral.

Statement of Values

Non Sibi

We strive to embody the ideal of *non sibi*, (not for self) with intentional teaching, learning, and engagement guided by a sense of responsibility toward the global community and natural world.

Youth from Every Quarter

We are committed to creating an equitable and inclusive school in which students from diverse backgrounds, cultures, and experiences—including race, ethnicity, nationality, gender, socioeconomic class, sexual orientation, gender identity, religion, and ability—learn and grow together.

Knowledge and Goodness

We challenge students in mind, body, and spirit such that they may pursue the knowledge, develop the skills, and sustain the integrity needed to lead a responsible, fulfilling life.

A Vision of the Academic Program

In its 1778 constitution, Phillips Academy is charged with ensuring its students learn "the great end and real business of living." Inspired by this charge, we seek to cultivate in our students the capacities—among them analytical rigor, imaginative thought, and nuanced skepticism— necessary to identify and attain a great and worthy end: human flourishing. Our founders knew that adolescence is formative. By introducing our students to the diversity of human experience and to the complexities of the natural world, we push them to understand the world as it is. By fostering their abilities to question beliefs, systems, and the ways things are done, we press them to envision the world they seek to create.

To prepare its students for life in the world, Phillips Academy offers a liberal education. Oriented to all aspects of human experience, liberal education affirms that knowledge is intrinsically good and denies that education terminates with technical skill or professional success. Resisting specialization in favor of breadth, it initiates students into connected fields of understanding and prepares them to lead lives characterized by learning and understanding, responsibility and freedom.

The practice of responsibility and freedom demands that citizens have dispositions of the critical mind to recognize fact and valid argument and to comprehend the implications of the knowledge they produce and the things they create. It requires that citizens act against intolerance and injustice and build communities conducive to human flourishing. To help students become such citizens, Phillips Academy seeks to prepare graduates who are educated broadly, discerning of ideologies, and committed to the public good.

Abbreviations

CLASS	Classroom Assessment Scoring System
COVID-19	coronavirus disease 2019
ERIC	Education Resources Information Center
K–12	kindergarten through 12th grade
NEASC	New England Association of Schools and Colleges
STEM	science, technology, engineering, and mathematics

References

Adelman, Clifford, *To Imagine a Verb: The Language and Syntax of Learning Outcomes Statements*, National Institute for Learning Outcomes Assessment, Occasional Paper No. 24, 2015.

Agency for Healthcare Research and Quality, "CAHPS Bibliography," webpage, undated. As of October 15, 2022: https://www.ahrq.gov/cahps/bibliography/index.html

Andrade, Maureen Snow, "Learning Gain: A U.S. Perspective," *Higher Education Pedagogies*, Vol. 3, No. 1, 2018.

Archer, Jeff, Steve Cantrell, Steven L. Holtzman, Jilliam N. Joe, Cynthia M. Tocci, and Jess Wood, *Better Feedback for Better Teaching: A Practical Guide to Improving Classroom Observations*, Bill & Melinda Gates Foundation, 2016.

Archibald, Sarah, Jane G. Coggshall, Andrew Croft, and Laura Goe, *High-Quality Professional Development for All Teachers: Effectively Allocating Resources*, National Comprehensive Center for Teacher Quality, 2011.

Armstrong, P., "Bloom's Taxonomy," Vanderbilt University Center for Teaching, 2010. As of October 7, 2022: https://cft.vanderbilt.edu/guides-sub-pages/blooms-taxonomy/

Bandura, A, *Social Foundations of Thought and Action: A Social-Cognitive View*, Prentice Hall, 1986.

Beiderbeck, Daniel, Nicolas Frevel, Heiko A. von der Gracht, Sascha L. Schmidt, and Vera M. Schweitzer, "Preparing, Conducting, and Analyzing Delphi Surveys: Cross-Disciplinary Practices, New Directions, and Advancements," *MethodsX*, Vol. 8, 2021.

Bell, Amani, and Kate Thomson, "Supporting Peer Observation of Teaching: Collegiality, Conversations, and Autonomy," *Innovations in Education and Teaching International*, Vol. 55, No. 3, 2018.

Bell, Maureen, and Paul Cooper, "Peer Observation of Teaching in University Departments: A Framework for Implementation," *International Journal for Academic Development*, Vol. 18, No. 1, 2013.

Berliner, David C., "Between Scylla and Charybdis: Reflections on and Problems Associated with the Evaluation of Teachers in an Era of Metrification," *Education Policy Analysis Archives*, Vol. 26, No. 54, 2018.

Bernard, H. Russell, Amber Wutich, and Gery W. Ryan, *Analyzing Qualitative Data: Systematic Approaches*, Sage Publications, 2016.

Berner, Ashley, *Would School Inspections Work in the United States?* Johns Hopkins School of Education, Institute for Education Policy, 2017.

Bester, Marianne, and Desireé Scholtz, "Mapping Our Way to Coherence, Alignment and Responsiveness," *South African Journal of Higher Education*, Vol. 26, No. 2, 2012.

Blazar, David, "Teacher Coaching to Improve Instruction at Scale: Opportunities and Challenges in Policy Contexts," *Teachers College Record*, Vol. 122, No. 10, 2020.

Bohen, Shawn Jacqueline, and James Stiles, "Experimenting with Models of Faculty Collaboration: Factors That Promote Their Success," *New Directions for Institutional Research*, Vol. 1998, No. 100, 1998.

Boring, Anne, Kellie Ottoboni, and Philip Stark, "Student Evaluations of Teaching (Mostly) Do Not Measure Teaching Effectiveness," *ScienceOpen Research*, 2016.

Campbell, Shanyce L., and Matthew Ronfeldt, "Observational Evaluation of Teachers: Measuring More Than We Bargained for?" *American Educational Research Journal*, Vol. 55, No. 6, 2018.

Casabianca, J. M., J. R. Lockwood, and D. F. McCaffrey, "Trends in Classroom Observation Scores," *Education and Psychological Measurement*, Vol. 75, No. 2, April 2015.

Chance, Beth, and Roxy Peck, "From Curriculum Guidelines to Learning Outcomes: Assessment at the Program Level," *American Statistician*, Vol. 69, No. 4, 2015.

Chaplin, Duncan, Brian Gill, Allison Thompkins, and Hannah Miller, *Professional Practice, Student Surveys, and Value-Added: Multiple Measures of Teacher Effectiveness in the Pittsburgh Public Schools*, Regional Educational Laboratory Mid-Atlantic, REL 2014-024, 2014.

Cherasaro, Trudy L., R. Marc Brodersen, Marianne L. Reale, and David C. Yanoski, *Teachers' Responses to Feedback from Evaluators: What Feedback Characteristics Matter?* Regional Educational Laboratory Central, REL 2017-190, 2016.

Clayton, Mark J., "Delphi: A Technique to Harness Expert Opinion for Critical Decision-Making Tasks in Education," *Educational Psychology*, Vol. 17, No. 4, 1997.

Close, Kevin, Audrey Amrein-Beardsley, and Clarin Collins, "Putting Teacher Evaluation Systems on the Map: An Overview of State's Teacher Evaluation Systems Post-Every Student Succeeds Act," *Education Policy Analysis Archives*, Vol. 28, No. 58, 2020.

Coggshall, Jane G., Claudette Rasmussen, Amy Colton, Jessica Milton, and Catherine Jacques, *Generating Teaching Effectiveness: The Role of Job-Embedded Professional Learning in Teacher Evaluation*, National Comprehensive Center for Teacher Quality, May 2012.

Cohen, Julie, and Dan Goldhaber, "Building a More Complete Understanding of Teacher Evaluation Using Classroom Observations," *Educational Researcher*, Vol. 45, No. 6, 2016.

Cook, Clayton R., Aaron R. Lyon, Jill Locke, Thomas Waltz, and Byron J. Powell, "Adapting a Compilation of Implementation Strategies to Advance School-Based Implementation Research and Practice," *Prevention Science*, Vol. 20, No. 6, 2019.

Copland, Michael A., "Leadership of Inquiry: Building and Sustaining Capacity for School Improvement," *Educational Evaluation and Policy Analysis*, Vol. 25, No. 4, 2003.

Cormas, Peter C., Gregg Gould, Louise Nicholson, Kyle C. Fredrick, and S. Y. Doan, "A Professional Development Framework for Higher Education Science Faculty That Improves Student Learning," *BioScience*, Vol. 71, No. 9, September 2021.

Dalal, Siddhartha R., Dmitry Khodyakov, Ramesh Srinivasan, Susan G. Straus, and John Adams, "ExpertLens: A System for Eliciting Opinions from a Large Pool of Non-Collocated Experts with Diverse Knowledge," *Technological Forecasting and Social Change*, Vol. 78, No. 8, 2011.

Dalkey, Norman, and Olaf Helmer, "An Experimental Application of the DELPHI Method to the Use of Experts," *Management Science*, Vol. 9, No. 3, 1963.

Datnow, Amanda, and Marisa Eileen Castellano, "Managing and Guiding School Reform: Leadership in Success for All Schools," *Educational Administration Quarterly*, Vol. 37, No. 2, 2001.

Denzin, Norman K., ed., *Sociological Methods: A Sourcebook*, 1st ed., Routledge, 2006.

Denzin, Norman K., and Yvonna S. Lincoln, *Collecting and Interpreting Qualitative Materials*, 2nd ed., Sage Publications, 2003.

Desimone, Laura, "How Can Comprehensive School Reform Models Be Successfully Implemented?" *Review of Educational Research*, Vol. 72, No. 3, 2002.

Desimone, Laura M., "Improving Impact Studies of Teachers' Professional Development: Toward Better Conceptualizations and Measures," *Educational Researcher*, Vol. 38, No. 3, 2009.

Doan, Sy, Lucas Greer, Heather L. Schwartz, Elizabeth D. Steiner, and Ashley Woo, *State of the American Teacher and State of the American Principal Surveys: 2022 Technical Documentation and Survey Results*, RAND Corporation, RR-A1108-3, 2022. As of October 7, 2022:
https://www.rand.org/pubs/research_reports/RRA1108-3.html

Dyjur, Patti, and Frances Kalu, *Introduction to Curriculum Review*, Taylor Institute for Teaching and Learning, University of Calgary, 2016.

Dyjur, Patti, and Jennifer Lock, "A Model to Build Capacity Through a Multi-Program Curriculum Review Process," *Journal of Professional, Continuing, and Online Education*, Vol. 2, No. 1, 2016.

Dynarski, Mark, "Teacher Observations Have Been a Waste of Time and Money," *Education Next*, December 12, 2016.

Ehren, Melanie C. M., Herbert Altrichter, Gerry McNamara, and Joe O'Hara, "Impact of School Inspections on Improvement of Schools: Describing Assumptions On Causal Mechanisms in Six European Countries," *Educational Assessment, Evaluation and Accountability*, Vol. 25, No. 1, 2013.

Ehren, Melanie C. M., Jan-Eric Gustafsson, Herbert Altrichter, Guri Skedsmo, David Kemethofer, and Stephan G. Huber, "Comparing Effects and Side Effects of Different School Inspection Systems Across Europe," *Comparative Education*, Vol. 51, No. 3, 2015.

Ehren, Melanie C. M., and Adrie J. Visscher, "The Relationships Between School Inspections, School Characteristics and School Improvement," *British Journal of Educational Studies*, Vol. 56, No. 2, 2008.

Elmore, Richard F., "Backward Mapping: Implementation Research and Policy Decisions," *Political Science Quarterly*, Vol. 94, No. 4, 1979.

English, David, Jackie Burniske, Debra Meibaum, and Lisa Lachlan-Haché, *Uncommon Measures: Student Surveys and Their Use in Measuring Teaching Effectiveness*, American Institutes for Research, 2015.

Ervin, Lesley, Bronwyn Carter, and Priscilla Robinson, "Curriculum Mapping: Not as Straightforward as It Sounds," *Journal of Vocational Education and Training*, Vol. 65, No. 3, 2013.

Fan, Yanan, Laura J. Shepherd, Eve Slavich, David Waters, M. Stone, Rachel Abel, and Emma L. Johnston, "Gender and Cultural Bias in Student Evaluations: Why Representation Matters," *PLoS One*, Vol. 14, No. 2, 2019.

Feeney, Eric J, "Quality Feedback: The Essential Ingredient for Teacher Success," *The Clearing House: A Journal of Educational Strategies, Issues and Ideas*, Vol. 80, No. 4, 2007.

Ferlazzo, Larry, "Throw Out the Protocol for Teacher Observations. Use Common Sense Instead," *EducationWeekly*, February 15, 2022.

Fitch, Kathryn, Steven J. Bernstein, Maria Dolores Aguilar, Bernard Burnand, Juan Ramon LaCalle, Pablo Lazaro, Mirjam van het Loo, Joseph McDonnell, Janneke Vader, and James P. Kahan, *The RAND/UCLA Appropriateness Method User's Manual*, RAND Corporation, MR-1269-DG-XII/RE, 2001. As of August 02, 2022: https://www.rand.org/pubs/monograph_reports/MR1269.html

Fleenor, John W., "What Can We Learn from Research on Multisource Feedback in Organizations?" in Wolfram Rollett, Hannah Bijlsma, and Sebastian Rhol, eds., *Student Feedback on Teaching in Schools: Using Student Perceptions for the Development of Teaching and Teachers*, Springer, 2021.

Fletcher, Jeffrey A., "Peer Observation of Teaching: A Practical Tool in Higher Education," *Journal of Faculty Development*, Vol. 32, No. 1, 2018.

Flowers, Nancy, Steven B. Mertens, and Peter F. Mulhall, "Teacher Views on Collaborative Review of Student Work," *Middle School Journal*, Vol. 37, No. 2, 2005.

Furco, Andrew, and Barbara E. Moely, "Using Learning Communities to Build Faculty Support for Pedagogical Innovation: A Multi-Campus Study," *Journal of Higher Education*, Vol. 83, No. 1, 2012.

Garet, Michael S., Andrew C. Porter, Laura Desimone, Beatrice F. Birman, and Kwang Suk Yoon, "What Makes Professional Development Effective? Results from a National Sample of Teachers," *American Educational Research Journal*, Vol. 38, No. 4, 2001.

Garubo, Raymond C., and Stanley William Rothstein, *Supportive Supervision in Schools*, Greenwood Publishing Group, 1998.

Gast, I., K. Schildkamp, and J. T. van der Veen, "Team-Based Professional Development Interventions in Higher Education: A Systematic Review," *Review of Educational Research*, Vol. 87, No. 4, August 2017.

Geiger, Tray, and Audrey Amrein-Beardsley, "Student Perception Surveys for K–12 Teacher Evaluation in the United States: A Survey of Surveys," *Cogent Education*, Vol. 6, No. 1, 2019.

Gibbons, Lynsey K., and Paul Cobb, "Focusing on Teacher Learning Opportunities to Identify Potentially Productive Coaching Activities," *Journal of Teacher Education*, Vol. 68, No. 4, 2017.

Gill, Brian, Megan Shoji, Thomas Coen, Kate Place, Mid-Atlantic Regional Educational Laboratory, I. C. F. International, Evaluation National Center for Education, and Assistance Regional, *The Content, Predictive Power, and Potential Bias in Five Widely Used Teacher Observation Instruments*, Regional Educational Laboratory Mid-Atlantic, REL 2017-191, 2016.

Göbel, Kerstin, Corinne Wyss, Katharina Neuber, and Meike Raaflaub, "Student Feedback as a Source for Reflection in Practical Phases of Teacher Education," in Wolfram Rollett, Hannah Bijlsma, and Sebastian Rhol, eds., *Student Feedback on Teaching in Schools: Using Student Perceptions for the Development of Teaching and Teachers*, Springer, 2021.

Göllner, Richard, Benjamin Fauth, and Wolfgang Wagner, "Student Ratings of Teaching Quality Dimensions: Empirical Findings and Future Directions," in Wolfram Rollett, Hannah Bijlsma, and Sebastian Rhol, eds., *Student Feedback on Teaching in Schools: Using Student Perceptions for the Development of Teaching and Teachers*, Springer, 2021.

Gosling, David, "Models of Peer Observation of Teaching," LTSN Generic Centre, August 2002.

Gravestock, Pamela, and Emily Gregor-Greenleaf, *Student Course Evaluations: Research, Models and Trends*, Citeseer, 2008.

Greatorex, Jackie, Nicky Rushton, Tori Coleman, Ellie Darlington, Gill Elliott, and Assessment Cambridge, *Towards a Method for Comparing Curricula*, Cambridge Assessment, 2019.

Greenfield, Victoria A., Sandra Kay Evans, Laura Werber, Samantha Cherney, and Lisa Pelled Colabella, *Performance Management and Assessment of Federally Funded Research and Development Centers: Lessons from Academic Literature and Practitioner Guidance*, RAND Corporation, RR-A737-2, 2022. As of October 20, 2022: https://www.rand.org/pubs/research_reports/RRA737-2.html

Grissom, Jason A, and Brendan Bartanen, "Potential Race and Gender Biases in High-Stakes Teacher Observations," *Journal of Policy Analysis and Management*, Vol. 41, No. 1, 2022.

Hammersley-Fletcher, Linda, and Paul Orsmond, "Evaluating Our Peers: Is Peer Observation a Meaningful Process?" *Studies in Higher Education*, Vol. 29, No. 4, 2004.

Hanna, Rema N., and Leigh L. Linden, "Discrimination in Grading," *American Economic Journal: Economic Policy*, Vol. 4, No. 4, 2012.

Harden, Ronald M., "AMEE Guide No. 21: Curriculum Mapping: A Tool for Transparent and Authentic Teaching and Learning," *Medical Teacher*, Vol. 23, No. 2, 2001.

Hardre, Patricia, "Checked Your Bias Lately? Reasons and Strategies for Rural Teachers to Self-Assess for Grading Bias," *Rural Educator*, Vol. 35, No. 2, 2014.

Harvey, Lee, "An Assessment of Past and Current Approaches to Quality in Higher Education," *Australian Journal of Education*, Vol. 42, No. 3, 1998.

Hinnerich, Björn Tyrefors, Erik Höglin, and Magnus Johannesson, "Are Boys Discriminated in Swedish High Schools?" *Economics of Education Review*, Vol. 30, No. 4, 2011.

Ho, Andrew, and Thomas Kane, *The Reliability of Classroom Observations by School Personnel*, Bill & Melinda Gates Foundation, January 2013.

Hornstein, Henry A., "Student Evaluations of Teaching are an Inadequate Assessment Tool for Evaluating Faculty Performance," *Cogent Education*, Vol. 4, No. 1, 2017.

Hudson, Eric, *Designing a Graduate Profile: Four Essential Steps*, Global Online Academy, November 13, 2019.

Hunter, Seth B., and Matthew G. Springer, "Critical Feedback Characteristics, Teacher Human Capital, and Early-Career Teacher Performance: A Mixed-Methods Analysis," *Educational Evaluation and Policy Analysis*, Vol. 44, No. 3, 2022.

Hussain, Iftikhar, "Subjective Performance Evaluation in the Public Sector Evidence from School Inspections," *Journal of Human Resources*, Vol. 50, No. 1, 2015.

Jacobsen, Michele, Sarah Elaine Eaton, Barb Brown, Marlon Simmons, and Mairi McDermott, "Action Research for Graduate Program Improvements: A Response to Curriculum Mapping and Review," *Canadian Journal of Higher Education*, Vol. 48, No. 1, 2018.

Jankowski, Natasha A., Jennifer D. Timmer, Jillian Kinzie, and George D. Kuh, *Assessment That Matters: Trending Toward Practices That Document Authentic Student Learning*, National Institute for Learning Outcomes Assessment, 2018.

Jerald, Craig D., "On Her Majesty's School Inspection Service," *Educator Sector*, Vol. 8, 2012.

Jilani, Shahla M., Hendrée E. Jones, Matthew Grossman, Lauren M. Jansson, Mishka Terplan, Laura J. Faherty, Dmitry Khodyakov, Stephen W. Patrick, and Jonathan M. Davis, "Standardizing the Clinical Definition of Opioid Withdrawal in the Neonate," *Journal of Pediatrics*, Vol. 243, 2022.

Joe, Jilliam N., Cynthia M. Tocci, Steven L Holtzman, and Jean C. Williams, *Foundations of Observation: Considerations for Developing a Classroom Observation System That Helps Districts Achieve Consistent and Accurate Scores*, Bill & Melinda Gates Foundation, MET Project, Policy and Practice Brief, 2013.

Kalogrides, Demetra, Susanna Loeb, and Tara Béteille, "Systematic Sorting: Teacher Characteristics and Class Assignments," *Sociology of Education*, Vol. 86, No. 2, 2013.

Kalu, Frances, and Patti Dyjur, "Creating a Culture of Continuous Assessment to Improve Student Learning through Curriculum Review," *New Directions for Teaching and Learning*, No. 155, 2018.

Kane, Thomas, and Steve Cantrell, *Learning About Teaching*, Bill & Melinda Gates Foundation, 2010.

Kane, Thomas J., and Douglas O. Staiger, *Gathering Feedback for Teaching: Combining High-Quality Observations with Student Surveys and Achievement Gains*, Bill & Melinda Gates Foundation, 2012.

Kang, Sung Pil, Yan Chen, Vanessa Svihla, Amber Gallup, Kristen Ferris, and Abhaya K. Datye, "Guiding Change in Higher Education: An Emergent, Iterative Application of Kotter's Change Model," *Studies in Higher Education*, Vol. 47, No. 2, 2022.

Kennedy, Declan, *Writing and Using Learning Outcomes: A Practical Guide*, University College Cork, 2006.

Kennedy, Declan, Áine Hyland, and Norma Ryan, "Learning Outcomes and Competences," *Introducing Bologna Objectives and Tools*, Vol. 3, 2009.

Kezar, Adrianna, and Elaine El-Khawas, "Using the Performance Dimension: Converging Paths for External Accountability," in Heather Eggins, ed., *Globalization and Reform in Higher Education*, Open University Press, 2003.

Khodyakov, Dmitry, Sean Grant, Brian Denger, Kathi Kinnett, Ann Martin, Marika Booth, Courtney Armstrong, Emily Dao, Christine Chen, Ian Coulter, Holly Peay, Glen Hazlewood, and Natalie Street, "Using an Online Modified-Delphi Approach to Engage Patients and Caregivers in Determining the Patient-Centeredness of Duchenne Muscular Dystrophy Care Considerations," *Medical Decision Making*, Vol. 39, No. 8, 2019.

Khodyakov, Dmitry, Sean Grant, Brian Denger, Kathi Kinnett, Ann Martin, Holly Peay, and Ian Coulter, "Practical Considerations in Using Online Modified-Delphi Approaches to Engage Patients and Other Stakeholders in Clinical Practice Guideline Development," *Patient-Centered Outcomes Research*, Vol. 13, No. 1, 2020.

Khodyakov, Dmitry, Susanne Hempel, Lisa Rubenstein, Paul Shekelle, Robbie Foy, Susanne Salem-Schatz, Sean O'Neill, Margie Danz, and Siddhartha Dalal, "Conducting Online Expert Panels: A Feasibility and Experimental Replicability Study," *BMC Medical Research Methodology*, Vol. 11, No. 1, 2011.

Khodyakov, Dmitry, Susan E. Stockdale, Nina Smith, Marika Booth, Lisa Altman, and Lisa V. Rubenstein, "Patient Engagement in the Process of Planning and Designing Outpatient Care Improvements at the Veterans Administration Health-Care System: Findings from an Online Expert Panel," *Health Expectations*, Vol. 20, No. 1, 2017.

Kim, Katherine K., Dmitry Khodyakov, Kate Marie, Howard Taras, Daniella Meeker, Hugo O. Campos, and Lucila Ohno-Machado, "A Novel Stakeholder Engagement Approach for Patient-Centered Outcomes Research," *Medical Care*, Vol. 56, 2018.

Kopera-Frye, Karen, John Mahaffy, and Gloria Messick Svare, "The Map to Curriculum Alignment and Improvement," *CELT*, Vol. 1, 2008.

Kraft, Matthew A., David Blazar, and Dylan Hogan, "The Effect of Teacher Coaching on Instruction and Achievement: A Meta-Analysis of the Causal Evidence," *Review of Educational Research*, Vol. 88, No. 4, August 2018.

Kraft, Matthew A., and Alvin Christian, "Can Teacher Evaluation Systems Produce High-Quality Feedback? An Administrator Training Field Experiment," *American Educational Research Journal*, Vol. 59, No. 3, 2021.

Kreitzer, Rebecca J., and Jennie Sweet-Cushman, "Evaluating Student Evaluations Of Teaching: A Review of Measurement and Equity Bias in SETs and Recommendations for Ethical Reform," *Journal of Academic Ethics*, Vol. 20, 2021.

Langer, Georgea M., Amy B. Colton, and Loretta S. Goff, *Collaborative Analysis of Student Work: Improving Teaching and Learning*, ASCD, 2003.

Levine, Thomas H., and Alan S. Marcus, "How the Structure and Focus of Teachers' Collaborative Activities Facilitate and Constrain Teacher Learning," *Teaching and Teacher Education*, Vol. 26, No. 3, 2010.

Lincoln, Yvonna S., and Egon G. Guba, *Naturalistic Inquiry*, Sage Publications, 1985.

Lindholm, Jennifer A., *Guidelines for Developing and Assessing Student Learning Outcomes for Undergraduate Majors*, Univeristy of California, Los Angeles, 2009.

Linse, Angela R., "Interpreting and Using Student Ratings Data: Guidance for Faculty Serving as Administrators and on Evaluation Committees," *Studies in Educational Evaluation*, Vol. 54, 2017.

MacNell, Lillian, Adam Driscoll, and Andrea N. Hunt, "What's in a Name: Exposing Gender Bias in Student Ratings of Teaching," *Innovative Higher Education*, Vol. 40, No. 4, 2015.

Malouff, John, "Bias in Grading," *College Teaching*, Vol. 56, No. 3, 2008.

Martin, Graham A., and Jeremy M. Double, "Developing Higher Education Teaching Skills Through Peer Observation and Collaborative Reflection," *Innovations in Education and Training International*, Vol. 35, No. 2, 1998.

McKeachie, Wilbert J., "Research on College Teaching: The Historical Background," *Journal of Educational Psychology*, Vol. 82, No. 2, 1990.

Meade, Adam W., and S. Bartholomew Craig, "Identifying Careless Responses in Survey Data," *Psychological Methods*, Vol. 17, No. 3, 2012.

Mengel, Friederike, Jan Sauermann, and Ulf Zölitz, "Gender Bias in Teaching Evaluations," *Journal of the European Economic Association*, Vol. 17, No. 2, 2019.

Miles, Matthew B., and A. Michael Huberman, *Qualitative Data Analysis: An Expanded Sourcebook*, 2nd ed., Sage Publications, 1994.

Nelson, Tamara, David Slavit, Mart Perkins, and Tom Hathorn, "A Culture of Collaborative Inquiry: Learning to Develop and Support Professional Learning Communities," *Teachers College Record*, Vol. 110, No. 6, 2008.

Newmann, Fred M., BetsAnn Smith, Elaine Allensworth, and Anthony S. Bryk, "Instructional Program Coherence: What It Is and Why It Should Guide School Improvement Policy," *Educational Evaluation and Policy Analysis*, Vol. 23, No. 4, 2001.

Newton, Jethro, "Feeding the Beast or Improving Quality? Academics' Perceptions of Quality Assurance and Quality Monitoring," *Quality in Higher Education*, Vol. 6, No. 2, 2000.

O'Connell, Brendan, Paul De Lange, Mark Freeman, Phil Hancock, Anne Abraham, Bryan Howieson, and Kim Watty, "Does Calibration Reduce Variability in the Assessment of Accounting Learning Outcomes?" *Assessment & Evaluation in Higher Education*, Vol. 41, No. 3, 2016.

Papay, John, "Refocusing the Debate: Assessing the Purposes and Tools of Teacher Evaluation," *Harvard Educational Review*, Vol. 82, No. 1, Spring 2012.

Peterson, David A. M., Lori A. Biederman, David Andersen, Tessa M. Ditonto, and Kevin Roe, "Mitigating Gender Bias in Student Evaluations of Teaching," *PLoS One*, Vol. 14, No. 5, 2019.

Poglinco, Susan M., Amy J. Bach, Kate Hovde, Sheila Rosenblum, Marisa Saunders, and Jonathan A. Supovitz, *The Heart of the Matter: The Coaching Model in America's Choice Schools*, CPRE Research Reports, 2003.

Polikoff, Morgan, Elaine Lin Wang, Shira Korn Haderlein, Julia H. Kaufman, Ashley Woo, Daniel Silver, and V. Darleen Opfer, *Exploring Coherence in English Language Arts Instructional Systems in the Common Core Era*, RAND Corporation, RR-A279-1, 2020. As of October 20, 2022:
https://www.rand.org/pubs/research_reports/RRA279-1.html

Popova, Anna, David K. Evans, Mary E. Breeding, and Violeta Arancibia, "Teacher Professional Development Around the World: The Gap Between Evidence and Practice," *World Bank Research Observer*, Vol. 37, No. 1, 2022.

Prado Tuma, Andrea, Laura S. Hamilton, and Tiffany Tsai, *A Nationwide Look at Teacher Perceptions of Feedback and Evaluation Systems: Findings from the American Teacher Panel*, RAND Corporation, RR-2558-BMGF, 2018. As of October 20, 2022:
https://www.rand.org/pubs/research_reports/RR2558.html

Provezis, Staci, *Regional Accreditation and Student Learning Outcomes: Mapping the Territory*, National Institute for Learning Outcomes Assessment, October 2010.

Putman, Hannah, Kate Walsh, and Elizabeth Ross, *Making a Difference: Six Places Where Teacher Evaluation Systems are Getting Results*, National Council on Teacher Quality, October 2018.

Rauschenberg, Samuel, "How Consistent Are Course Grades? An Examination of Differential Grading," *Education Policy Analysis Archives*, Vol. 22, No. 92, 2014.

Rawle, Fiona, Tracey Bowen, Barbara Murck, and Rosa Junghwa Hong, "Curriculum Mapping across the Disciplines: Differences, Approaches, and Strategies," *Collected Essays on Learning and Teaching*, Vol. 10, 2017.

Richardson, John T.E., "Instruments for Obtaining Student Feedback: A Review of the Literature," *Assessment & Evaluation in Higher Education*, Vol. 30, No. 4, 2005.

Robertson, Margaret, Martin Line, Susan Jones, and Sharon Thomas, "International Students, Learning Environments and Perceptions: A Case Study Using the Delphi Technique," *Higher Education Research and Development*, Vol. 19, No. 1, 2000.

Röhl, Sebastian, and Holger Gärtner, "Relevant Conditions for Teachers' Use of Student Feedback," in Wolfram Rollett, Hannah Bijlsma, and Sebastian Rhol, eds., *Student Feedback on Teaching in Schools: Using Student Perceptions for the Development of Teaching and Teachers*, Springer, 2021.

Rollett, Wolfram, Hannah Bijlsma, and Sebastian Röhl, "Student Feedback on Teaching in Schools: Current State of Research and Future Perspectives," in Rollett, Wolfram, Hannah Bijlsma, and Sebastian Röhl, eds., *Student Feedback on Teaching in Schools: Using Student Perceptions for the Development of Teaching and Teachers*, Springer, 2021.

Ross, Elizabeth, and Kate Walsh, *State of the States 2019: Teacher and Principal Evaluation Policy*, National Council on Teacher Quality, 2019.

Rothman, Robert, *School Quality Reviews: Promoting Accountability for Deeper Learning. Students at the Center: Deeper Learning Research Series*, Jobs for the Future, 2018.

Ryan, Gery W., and H. Russell Bernard, "Techniques to Identify Themes," *Field Methods*, Vol. 15, No. 1, February 2003.

Sachs, Judyth, and Mitch Parsell, *Peer Review of Learning and Teaching in Higher Education: International Perspectives*, Vol. 9, Springer Science and Business Media, 2013.

Schillemans, Thomas, "Does Horizontal Accountability Work? Evaluating Potential Remedies for the Accountability Deficit of Agencies," *Administration and Society*, Vol. 43, No. 4, 2011.

Schoepp, Kevin, "The State of Course Learning Outcomes at Leading Universities," *Studies in Higher Education*, Vol. 44, No. 4, 2019.

Schoepp, Kevin, Maurice Danaher, and Ashley Ater Kranov, "An Effective Rubric Norming Process," *Practical Assessment, Research, and Evaluation*, Vol. 23, No. 1, 2018.

Schutte, Kelli, David Line, and Chris McCullick, "Using Curriculum Mapping and Visualization to Maximize Effective Change," *Administrative Issues Journal: Connecting Education, Practice, and Research*, Vol. 8, No. 2, 2018.

Schweig, Jonathan, *Measuring Teacher Effectiveness: Understanding Common, Uncommon, and Combined Methods*, RAND Corporation, RR-4312/4, 2019. As of August 18, 2022:
https://www.rand.org/pubs/research_reports/RR4312z4.html

Schweig, Jonathan D., and José Felipe Martínez, "Understanding (Dis) Agreement in Student Ratings of Teaching and the Quality of the Learning Environment," in Wolfram Rollett, Hannah Bijlsma, and Sebastian Rhol, eds., *Student Feedback on Teaching in Schools: Using Student Perceptions for the Development of Teaching and Teachers*, Springer, 2021.

Shah, Mahsood, "Ten Years of External Quality Audit in Australia: Evaluating Its Effectiveness and Success," *Assessment & Evaluation in Higher Education*, Vol. 37, No. 6, 2012.

Shaw, Ian, Douglas P Newton, Murray Aitkin, and Ross Darnell, "Do OFSTED Inspections of Secondary Schools Make a Difference to GCSE results?" *British Educational Research Journal*, Vol. 29, No. 1, 2003.

Silva, Moisés, Ricardo Reich, and Gricelda Gallegos, "Effects of External Quality Evaluation in Chile: A Preliminary Study," *Quality in Higher Education*, Vol. 3, No. 1, 1997.

Smith, Austin F. R., and Vincent J. Fortunato, "Factors Influencing Employee Intentions to Provide Honest Upward Feedback Ratings," *Journal of Business and Psychology*, Vol. 22, No. 3, 2008.

Stecher, Brian M., Frank Camm, Cheryl L. Damberg, Laura S. Hamilton, Kathleen J. Mullen, Christopher Nelson, Paul Sorensen, Martin Wachs, Allison Yoh, Gail L. Zellman, and Kristin J. Leuschner, *Toward a Culture of Consequences: Performance-Based Accountability Systems for Public Services*, RAND Corporation, MG-1019, 2010. As of August 18, 2022:
https://www.rand.org/pubs/monographs/MG1019.html

Stecher, Brian M., Deborah J. Holtzman, Michael S. Garet, Laura S. Hamilton, John Engberg, Elizabeth D. Steiner, Abby Robyn, Matthew D. Baird, Italo A. Gutierrez, Evan D. Peet, Iliana Brodziak de los Reyes, Kaitlin Fronberg, Gabriel Weinberger, Gerald P. Hunter, and Jay Chambers, *Improving Teaching Effectiveness: Final Report: The Intensive Partnerships for Effective Teaching Through 2015–2016*, RAND Corporation, RR-2242-BMGF, 2018. As of August 18, 2022:
https://www.rand.org/pubs/research_reports/RR2242.html

Steinberg, Matthew, and Lauren Sartain, "What Explains the Race Gap in Teacher Performance Ratings? Evidence from Chicago Public Schools," *Educational Evaluation and Policy Analysis*, Vol. 43, No. 1, 2021.

Steinberg, Matthew P., and Rachel Garrett, "Classroom Composition and Measured Teacher Performance: What Do Teacher Observation Scores Really Measure?" *Educational Evaluation and Policy Analysis*, Vol. 38, No. 2, 2016.

Storage, Daniel, Zachary Horne, Andrei Cimpian, and Sarah-Jane Leslie, "The Frequency of "Brilliant" and "Genius" in Teaching Evaluations Predicts the Representation of Women and African Americans Across Fields," *PLoS One*, Vol. 11, No. 3, 2016.

Strauss, Anselm, and Juliet Corbin, "Grounded Theory Methodology: An Overview," in Norman K. Denzin and Yvonna S. Lincoln, eds., *Handbook of Qualitative Research*, 1st ed., Sage Publications, 1993.

Svinicki, Marilla D., "Encouraging Your Students to Give Feedback," *New Directions for Teaching and Learning*, Vol. 2001, No. 87, 2001.

Theall, Michael, and Jennifer Franklin, "Creating Responsive Student Rating Systems to Improve Evaluation Practice," *New Directions for Teaching and Learning*, Vol. 83, 2000.

Theall, Michael, and Jennifer Franklin, "Looking for Bias in all the Wrong Places: A Search for Truth or a Witch Hunt in Student Ratings of Instruction?" *New Directions for Institutional Research*, Vol. 2001, No. 109, 2001.

Timperley, Helen, *Professional Conversations and Improvement-Focused Feedback: A Review of the Research Literature and the Impact on Practice and Student Outcomes*, Australian Institute for Teaching and School Leadership, October 2015.

Torres, Amada, "Measuring Student Engagement Results from the 2015 High School Survey of Student Engagement," *Independent School*, Vol. 75, No. 4, 2016.

Trow, Martin, "Academic Reviews and the Culture of Excellence," University of California, Berkeley, working paper, 1994.

Uchiyama, Kay Pippin, and Jean L. Radin, "Curriculum Mapping in Higher Education: A Vehicle for Collaboration," *Innovative Higher Education*, Vol. 33, No. 4, 2009.

Uttl, Bob, "Lessons Learned from Research on Student Evaluation of Teaching in Higher Education," in Wolfram Rollett, Hannah Bijlsma, and Sebastian Rhol, eds., *Student Feedback on Teaching in Schools: Using Student Perceptions for the Development of Teaching and Teachers*, Springer, 2021.

Uttl, Bob, Carmela A. White, and Daniela Wong Gonzalez, "Meta-Analysis of Faculty's Teaching Effectiveness: Student Evaluation of Teaching Ratings and Student Learning Are Not Related," *Studies in Educational Evaluation*, Vol. 54, 2017.

Wang, Elaine Lin, Andrea Prado Tuma, Sy Doan, Daniella Henry, Rebecca Ann Lawrence, Ashley Woo, and Julia H. Kaufman, *Teachers' Perceptions of What Makes Instructional Materials Engaging, Appropriately Challenging, and Usable: A Survey and Interview Study*, RAND Corporation, RR-A134-2, 2021. As of August 18, 2022:
https://www.rand.org/pubs/research_reports/RRA134-2.html

Wang, Jue, George Engelhard Jr., Kevin Raczynski, Tian Song, and Edward W. Wolfe, "Evaluating Rater Accuracy and Perception for Integrated Writing Assessments Using a Mixed-Methods Approach," *Assessing Writing*, Vol. 33, 2017.

Waubonsee Community College, "Curriculum Maping," webpage, undated. As of October 25, 2022:
https://facultydae.waubonsee.edu/instruction/assessment/curriculum-mapping

Wayman, Jeffrey C., Steve Midgley, and Sam Stringfield, "Collaborative Teams to Support Data-Based Decision Making and Instructional Improvement," Annual Meeting of the American Educational Research Association, Montreal, Canada, 2005.

White, Andrew S., Michelle Howell Smith, Gina M. Kunz, and Gwen C. Nugent, *Active Ingredients of Instructional Coaching: Developing a Conceptual Framework*, National Center for Research on Rural Education, December 2015.

Whitlock, W., and Ann Rumpus, "Peer Observation: Collaborative Teaching Quality Enhancement," *Educational Initiative Centre Guide*, Vol. 5, 2004.

Wisniewski, Benedikt, and Klaus Zierer, "Functions and Success Conditions of Student Feedback in the Development of Teaching and Teachers," in Wolfram Rollett, Hannah Bijlsma, and Sebastian Rhol, eds., *Student Feedback on Teaching in Schools: Using Student Perceptions for the Development of Teaching and Teachers*, Springer, 2021.

Woulfin, Sarah L., "Crystallizing Coaching: An Examination of the Institutionalization of Instructional Coaching in Three Educational Systems," *Teachers College Record*, Vol. 122, No. 10, 2020.

Yoon, Kwang Suk, Teresa Duncan, Silvia Wen-Yu Lee, Beth Scarloss, and Kathy L. Shapley, *Reviewing the Evidence on How Teacher Professional Development Affects Student Achievement: Issues & Answers*, Regional Educational Laboratory Southwest, REL 2007-No. 033, 2007.

Yoon, Sun Young, "Principals' Data-Driven Practice and Its Influences on Teacher Buy-in and Student Achievement in Comprehensive School Reform Models," *Leadership and Policy in Schools*, Vol. 15, No. 4, 2016.

Zimmerman, Judith, "Why Some Teachers Resist Change and What Principals Can Do About It," *NASSP Bulletin*, Vol. 90, No. 3, 2006.

Ingram Content Group UK Ltd.
Milton Keynes UK
UKHW051009060423
419599UK00007B/30